GENESIS

GENESIS

A Latvian Childhood

Chaim Bermant

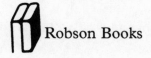 Robson Books

First published in Great Britain in 1998 by Robson
Books Ltd, Bolsover House, 5-6 Clipstone Street,
London W1P 8LE

British Library Cataloguing in Publication Data
A catalogue record for this title is available from the
British Library

ISBN 1 86105 175 1

Typeset in Plantin by FSH Print and Production Ltd,
London
Printed and bound by WBC, Bridgend, Mid Glam.

Foreword
by Judy Bermant

Chaim was at home in London putting the finishing touches to *Genesis* (Part One of his autobiographical memoir), when I phoned from Israel. 'Chaimke, it's me, Judy. Unbelievably, we have discovered Mendel Fleischman alive and well, living in Holon and I have just phoned him. He remembers all your family, especially your father, his beloved Reb Azriel. He also knows of other survivors from Barovke and would love to see you and speak with you.' I had been in tears while speaking to Mendel Fleischman but at this point, Chaim, Alisa (our eldest daughter who lives in Israel) and myself were crying and laughing at once. All of us in Israel had been involved one way or the other with research into the history of Jewish Barovke, Kreslavka and Breslev, where Chaim's family had lived before and up to the Second World War, when Chaim's immediate family left for Glasgow.

Chaim was impatient to get his book finished and as I was to be in Israel to celebrate my parents' Diamond Wedding anniversary, I told Chaim that I would use this opportunity to find out what I could from Yad Vashem in Jerusalem, the Diaspora Museum in Tel Aviv, and from other archival sources, to save him an unnecessary journey.

I would have preferred him to defer his trip till the summer when I could have accompanied him – and to contact everyone by phone and fax from London instead. In the event, Mendel Fleischman in person proved to be irresistible and Chaim more or less made plans on the spot to leave for Israel.

Genesis was to have been the first book of five charting Chaim's autobiographical journey through seventy-odd years of his life. He planned (as with the Israelites of old in the Pentateuch) to describe his journeyings: – from Latvia to Glasgow, from Thaxted (Essex) to Israel, to Sunderland, London and so on, and covering all the different stages, stories, travels, anecdotes that we have read about, thinly disguised in his novels, or heard about from Chaim himself and so many others.

I was uneasy, hesitant, though, about his leaving for Israel at this time, and Chaim knew it and booked his flight without telling me – till I overheard it in a telephone conversation with Alisa. In the light of subsequent events, I was right to be uneasy, for Chaim was not a man to look after himself. He smoked heavily, especially while writing. He suffered from high blood pressure, liver and cholesterol problems, and had a family history of heart disease (my late father-in-law died of a heart attack at our engagement). As his doctor put it, he was 'a walking time bomb'.

Everyone who saw him at this time in Israel spoke of his very high emotional state, his immense excitement at meeting up with so many survivors from his childhood, hearing their stories of their escape from the Nazis – and his turmoil at hearing first hand how Jewish Barovke met its end.

All the time he was also thinking about how to incorporate this new material into his book and meet his deadline, or whether to stay on longer and gather more material. When he phoned home to London, I could hear the intensity in his voice. I also heard him say that he felt unwell, how tired he was. and how much he was looking forward to coming home.

He arrived back in London on Sunday 18 January 1998, very unwell from the effects of gastroenteritis he picked up in Israel. He was ill all next day – too ill to think about writing his weekly *Jewish Chronicle* column, or anything else. Typically though, warned by his doctor to take only sips of water, he managed to stagger downstairs and find a beer when I wasn't looking. On Tuesday 20 January 1998 he died of suspected heart failure and without completing the epilogue to his book.

After the Shivah was over, we scanned his diary, notebooks and tape recorder but could find little to help us, only very brief notes mentioning names, a few dates ... and several photographs. So accordingly, Liz (my sister) and Alisa when back in Israel, retraced Chaim's footsteps and painstakingly pieced together all the information we needed. Of course, we couldn't incorporate this material into his manuscript, or adjust things here and there, as *he* might have done in the light of new information. We decided instead to include it at the end of the book as a kind of postscript.

Then we had to find the manuscript. Chaim had left it on the computer, edited but unprinted. I had seen him working on his autobiography for the past six months or so, but there was no manuscript to be seen. Consequently, as soon as the Shivah ended, we carefully searched through the entire contents of the hard disk. As we began the search, we all held our breath and only breathed easily again some hours later when our son, Danny, ran downstairs to say: 'We've found it! We've found it.' I was terrified that the files containing his work might have been deleted or damaged, but it was all intact.

It is so difficult to get a true perspective. Chaim achieved so much, yet he wanted to do so much more. He always hankered after a byline in a national newspaper, and would have thrived on the challenge of producing two quite diverse columns; it was the sort of challenge he needed. (For example, he would have loved to have taken on the Cassandra column in the *Daily Mirror*, after Bill Connor died.) He chafed at the constrictions placed on him by being categorized largely as a Jewish writer. He would have had such fun, given an opportunity, to tackle a wider variety of issues. Just think of what he might have written, for example, on the subject of President Clinton's 'social' life.

I feel terribly sad when I muse over the further books that will now never be written: the cobweb of vignettes, rich imagery, humour, stories always marvellously told in Chaim's inimitable voice, that would have taken us further into his life and into the life of family and friends. I *so* looked forward to being part of it all – with him. As it always was – with him.

This book is a unique testament to the Latvian childhood that Chaim and his sisters, Miriam and Sonja, often evoked and in some ways never left. In a way, Chaim was searching for it all his life. After reading his loving creation of a lost world, it is clear he completed the circle: growing up in Latvia and ending his life totally immersed in the memories and the recreation of his early childhood.

It seems to me that the nine-year-old boy who emerges from these pages is essentially the man I have always known and loved: bucolic and earthy, sometimes lonely and sad, with a wicked eye for detail, honest, knowledgeable, brutally incisive and yet so tender, so loving as well. Yet it is always a child's voice we hear, and again, Chaim was always childlike in a way. There was a freshness and innocence in his uncomplicated view of life. But he was also complex. He loved Jewish tradition, yet was critical of much in Jewish practice, was unsure about the Almighty but never sent off any copy without adding the Hebrew abbreviation 'By the grace of G–d' above it. He was a man of words yet often withdrawn, but also the unbelievably witty soul of any party. A large protective presence, yet so very vulnerable.

There is so very much more I would like to say: an unlimited stream of words that I could add to these already written. In the end I cannot sum him up – for he can't be pigeonholed. He was *sui generis*, and the world feels a much bleaker, paler shadow of itself for his absence.

'A man righteous and wholehearted in his generation'
Genesis VI, 9

Judy Bermant

Acknowledgements

Since Chaim was sadly unable to put the final touches to his manuscript, it fell to me – and a number of devoted helpers – to gather and organize the additional material which has been included in the postscript for this book.

I would like to thank the following people:

Danny Bermant, who found the missing manuscript after a thorough search of Chaim's word processor. Liz Olivestone and Alisa Bermant Karban for their interviews with Barovke survivors, and for meticulously checking the facts; Sonja Nemeth, for her amendments to the text, and Miriam Bermant, for lending her family photographs. The Yad Vashem Holocaust Museum and Mr Shlomo Kulanchik, of the Association of Latvian and Estonian Jews (Israel), for providing invaluable archive material – and Dr Leopold and Rachel Bayvel, Dr Abraham Pearlman and Azriel Bermant for their translations. Reuven Panz and Mendel Fleischman for sharing their memories of Barovke with us. Evie Bermant for compiling and editing the postscript material, Ruth Kelfa for her help with correcting the proofs. Sally Malnick, whose ancient Amstrad was responsible for Chaim's copious output in recent years, for her endless wisdom and practical help. Finally, my thanks must go to Jeremy and Carole Robson, (publishers) and to Kate Mills, the editor, for their advice, constant patience and sensitivity, and for their absolute conviction that Chaim wouldn't let them down.

Judy Bermant

A Note on Transliteration

There can be a risk of losing some local flavour when transliterating Yiddish into English, especially where Chaim Bermant is concerned. His rich language encompassed Latvian, Russian and Polish Yiddish which led to variations in spelling in certain expressions. Where this occurs, we felt it important to retain the author's original version.

We are grateful to the Oxford Institute for Yiddish Studies for their help in checking the many Yiddish expressions in this book and for their very valuable advice.

Preface

No man is on oath when writing his autobiography. I do not claim that every line I quote in direct speech was actually said in the way I said it. I would not even vouch for the authenticity of every detail I describe, but there are no fictional characters in this book, no contrived events, and no fabricated situations. I have tried to stick to the facts as I remember them.

And there's the rub; memories are faulty, especially where they touch on distant events, and the events described here took place between 1932–8 in a faraway country and almost everyone I have mentioned is dead.

Barovke* was not my birthplace but I spent some of my most formative years there and I first thought of writing a book about it some 30 years ago. My father, who was never particularly talkative, especially about the past, was dead by then. My mother, however, was still alive, and not a few of the incidents described in this book are drawn from her recollections. She never retained any papers or documents – other than my birth certificate – but she did have a sizeable collection of photographs and they helped to jog her memory, and mine. She died in 1971.

A year later I went to Russia in the hope of revisiting scenes of my childhood and although I was able to travel fairly extensively

---

*In official Russian sources, the village is often called Borovka but the Jewish/Yiddish pronunciation was Barovke.

I was not allowed to go anywhere near Latvia, let alone Barovke.

I was equipped with the addresses and, in some instances, the telephone numbers, of a number of Latvian Jews, including a cousin, who were said to be living in Moscow and Leningrad. Most of the addresses proved to be wrong, the few people I was able to contact had no wish to speak to me and, a trifle disheartened, I dropped the idea of the book, though I devoted a chapter to Barovke in *Coming Home*, a collection of autobiographical essays published in 1976.

As one grows older, however, and the future becomes attenuated, the past becomes more vivid, and especially the distant past, which does not, of course, mean that it becomes more accurate. If anything it becomes more fanciful and calls for careful appraisal and, where possible, external verification.

By 1990 Russia had become more open and I was able to visit both Latvia and Barovke, and although the Barovke I had known was no more, the lakes were still there and the forests, and the small wooden houses with their lopsided windows characteristic of the east European *shtetl*, and if I could summon no witnesses, I was able to confirm the topography of my boyhood years. I was also conscious of ghosts on every side, and the idea of a Barovke book was reborn.

I may have left it late. I have searched the memories of my two older sisters, but their recollections rarely tally with each other or mine, and not a few crucial details on which we all three agreed have proved to be wrong.

For example, we all believed that there were some three to four hundred Jews in Barovke, whereas according to the 1935 census, the true figure was only 189, or about 38 families. We also believed that though Barovke was small it was overwhelmingly Jewish. In fact, though Jews occupied the centre of the village they actually comprised less than a fifth of the population and, instead of being the compact little place we remembered, Barovke was scattered over a fairly wide area.

Given the Jewish aversion to being counted – which goes back to Biblical times – it is possible that the official figures are wrong, especially as there were Jews in Barovke who had no right to be there, having smuggled themselves over the border from Poland.

The small can look large to children, the young old and the few many, but I distinctly remember some 30 to 40 boys aged seven to 14 in the local Hebrew classes which, given normal demographic projections, would have suggested a Jewish population of at least 300. There were also three kosher butchers – I can remember them by name – and they could not have survived with only 189 customers between them, especially as few Jewish families could afford to eat meat on weekdays.

(The fact that there were also two synagogues is beside the point, for as legend has it, every Jew, apart from his usual house of prayer, needs another in which he will never set foot. I can only attest that I regularly attended both.)

When I was back in Barovke in 1990 I asked one of the very few people in the place who could recall the prewar years how many Jews there were in the village, and he said about 500, but he wasn't Jewish and Christians have always had an exaggerated idea of Jewish numbers. The one Jewish survivor I came across was an old communist who said he had nothing to do with the Jewish community and remembered nothing about it.

According to Professor Dov Levin's Pinkas Hakehillot, Barovke came into being in 1790, and grew slowly and erratically. By 1897 it had a population of about 700, including 285 Jews, and by 1914 Jews comprised more than half the population and derived a fairly comfortable livelihood from the timber trade.

The outbreak of war transformed their existence. The Jews were thought to be pro-German – given their experience under Tsarist rule, they had little reason to be pro-Russian – and, in 1915, together with other Jews in the vicinity, they were deported to Vitebsk in Byelorussia. They trickled back once the war was over and the community, as a community, was only revived in the course of the early twenties.

Barovke was by then cut off from the Russian hinterland which had provided many Jews with a livelihood. The more prosperous elements had moved on to the nearby city of Dvinsk, and most of the inhabitants were petty traders and artisans and a report made by a field team from the Jewish Distribution Committee paints a picture of poverty and hardship.

Numbers, however, continued to grow and by 1925 there were 265 Jews in Barovke, including 60 children of school age. The community acquired a full-time rabbi and opened a Jewish day school, and Barovke enjoyed a brief, very brief, and not very gilded, golden age. Thereafter the story is one of decline. The school closed, the rabbi left, and was succeeded by my father who functioned as a *shochet* (ritual slaughterer), cantor, teacher and general religious factotum, which is to say he performed all the duties of a rabbi without being paid for them, and derived his income from cutting throats.

By 1935, when there were only 189 Jews in Barovke out of a total population of over a thousand, Jews owned 17 of the 25 shops and warehouses in the village and the very fact that there were 38 households suggests a larger figure because families were large even where homes were small, and several generations sometimes lived together under one roof. I often wondered where they all slept.

Whatever the numbers, Barovke as a *shtetl* is no more. After Russia occupied the country in 1940 a few local Jews were deported with other Latvians to central Asia. The rest – and they comprised the overwhelming majority – were rounded up and slaughtered by the Germans and their Latvian auxiliaries in the nearby forest in the autumn of 1941. That forest was my playground.

But even if Barovke was as small as the official figures suggest, it featured hugely in my imagination and I describe it as I remember it.

I was born, however, in Breslev (known also as Braslav or Braslawa), which is described later. Part of this book concerns what might be called my prehistory and derives from incidents recalled by my mother and sisters. Father never spoke about Breslev – perhaps with good reason – but then he rarely said much about anything. For a rabbi, he was exceedingly sparing with words.

Breslev was the subject of a fascinating book, *Darkness and Desolation*, compiled by former residents of the town, which was

published in 1986. I read it from cover to cover in the hope that
it might refresh my memory, but it left me rather confused for the
town they describe bears little resemblance to the town I recall. As
they had lived there for years, while I was only there for months,
I have no doubt that their impressions are right and mine are
wrong, but I have nevertheless reserved the right to describe my
impressions ...

This, therefore, does not purport to be an authoritative account
of life in Barovke and Breslev in the thirties, but life as I
remember it, and I think I may be forgiven for sticking to my
version, if only as one testimony among others. Half a truth may
be worse than a whole lie, but something like a correct impression
can emerge from a collation of conflicting ones.

I was four when I came to Barovke, and nine when I left for
Glasgow. I was not precocious as a child, if anything I was
backward, but I had vast curiosity, would poke my nose into
everything and ask questions about everything, and retain a great
many vivid impressions which form the main body of this work
and which, if sometimes inaccurate in detail, are, I believe, true as
a whole.

In view of the tragic fate which eventually overtook Breslev,
Barovke – and every other *shtetl* in eastern Europe – some readers
may feel that I could have been gentler in my descriptions and
kinder in my remarks. 'All the dead are holy', goes an old Jewish
saying, but I am trying to evoke a living community, and where
there is life there is imperfection and the imperfections, in so far
as I remember them, were, in the main, forgivable. Moreover
people can be loved as much for their idiosyncrasies and defects,
as for their virtues. I recall them as I remember them and I like to
think that the underlying affection I had for them emerges from
this account.

My picture of Breslev was clouded by my own personal
unhappiness, but my unhappiness derived from my own peculiar
circumstances rather than from Breslev itself. This is a story with
few heroes, and no villains – well almost none.

To write an autobiography at all is a form of presumption; to
confine it to the first nine years of one's life is a form of

megalomania and my only excuse in writing this book is that I am not trying to recover my own story so much as the story of one small corner of a large world which has since vanished and which richly deserves to be commemorated.

'To die completely,' wrote Samuel Butler, 'a person must not only forget but be forgotten, and he who is not forgotten is not dead.' The same, I believe, applies to places.

Jewish Breslev is no more. A few survivors returned after the war but then moved on to Israel or America.

After Jewish Barovke was extirpated by the Nazis in 1941, what was left of it was transformed by the Russians after 1945. It is now no longer even a place on the map and has been absorbed by the nearby village of Skrudaliena.

Chapter 1

The Gang

The words *shtetl* and *shtetele* are both Yiddish, but have become so familiar that they are almost part of the English language.

They derive from *shtot*, which means town. *Shtetl* was thus a small town, and *shtetaleh*, a very small town, or village, though many a *shtot* was sometimes referred to affectionately as a *shtetl*, and many a *shtetl* as a *shtetaleh*.

Anything smaller than a *shtetele* was a *dorf*. But it was not merely a matter of size. Where a *dorf* had a Jewish community large enough to build a synagogue and employ a rabbi it acquired the dignity of a *shtetele*, much as an English town which becomes the seat of a bishop acquires the status of a city.

My father, who died in 1962, was the last rabbi of Barovke, a Latvian *shtetele* which he served from 1932 until he left for Glasgow in 1937. We followed a year or so later.

There is no early history of Latvia as Latvia. Different parts of the country were ruled at different times by different neighbours – Germans, Swedes, Poles – until the country as a whole was absorbed by Russia in the course of the eighteenth century. The Russian Revolution enabled Latvia to emerge from the shadows and it finally became independent in 1918, and was recognized as such at Versailles in 1919, though two or three years of chaos

1

ensued before it attained anything like stability.

The country is only about 25,000 square miles in size, or half the area of England, and about a fifth of it is covered by forest even now. It is sparsely populated with under three million inhabitants, of whom about a third live in the capital Riga, and is divided into three provinces, Kurland, Livonia and Latgale.

Of the three, Kurland with its large coastline was the most developed, and Latgale, which bordered on Russia and Poland, the most backward. The dominant cultural influence in the first two, even under Russian rule, was German, while Latgale was essentially Russian.

There is also no early history of Barovke. The First World War, the Russian Revolution, the Russian Civil War, the wars of the contending petty nationalities, had, like a raging typhoon, washed away entire communities and scattered them all over the great plains of eastern Europe like so many alluvial deposits. Barovke was one of them. Its Latvian name was Silene, but no one called it that, any more than one would call Dublin Baile Átha Cliath. It was a clearing in the forest near the Polish border, and I suspect it prospered because of the border. It was, however, a precarious prosperity. Some did well some of the time, a few did well most of the time, and more than a few did badly all of the time, though no one starved, if only because those who did badly had an immediate claim on those who did well.

Barovke consisted of a few dozen shops and houses, some neatly grouped round the small cobbled square, the rest scattered in all directions as if blown by the wind. The houses were built on high stone foundations to keep the timber above the level of the snows, with steep roofs and sagging windows, like unhappy eyes in an unhappy face. Doors, too sagged, as did shutters, and there was a built-in lopsidedness about the whole place. The more prosperous homes were brightly painted in red and yellow with white window frames. Many dwellings were set in small gardens or orchards, surrounded by an affected, tiny, brightly painted wooden fence, with the tops carved like the onion domes of a Russian church.

To the right of our house was Jan, or Janis, the village

policeman, and his wife Titania. Jan was a kindly man with a Hitler moustache, shaggy eyebrows, and a woebegone expression. As the local representative of authority he made authority seem benign.

So did Father, which is possibly why they became friends, though as the local rabbi he represented Higher Authority. If Jan was Caesar, father was God.

Jan's wife Titania looked as if she didn't quite belong to Barovke and felt as if she didn't. Mother felt the same, though, as I shall explain, they had other things in common, including a belief that they had married beneath them.

On our left was our landlord Chaim Ratz, tailor by profession – and a very good one – who also owned several houses and small plots of land in and around Barovke. He was a short, robust figure, with broad shoulders, round wire-rimmed glasses, a bushy moustache and a bushy beard. Beard and moustache overlapped and, as he rarely spoke, he looked mouthless.

He had a white-haired wife, Bashke, who was small, slight and tireless. She collected his rents, kept his accounts, tended his fields, fed the chickens, milked the goat, and kept house not only for her husband, but for their daughter-in-law, Hannah, whose house abutted on theirs.

Hannah Ratz, red-haired and with a milk-white skin, came from Dvinsk, and had never quite adapted herself to village life or, indeed, domestic life. She had two small, plump children and always looked as if she was about to bring forth a third, but somehow never did. According to her mother-in-law she had *tsvey linke hent und tsvey linke fis* – two left hands and two left feet. She couldn't clean, cook, sew or perform most of the other duties expected of a good Jewish housewife or even a bad one.

Hannah sounded as if she was complaining even when she said good morning and, in truth, she had a lot to complain about. She would come out in red blisters in the hot weather, and would be convulsed with shivers when it turned cold and in the winter she wore a fur coat and shawl indoors. Her huband Hannoch, a lean, dour, leathery figure, rarely spoke to her without raising his voice. Above all, she could not cope with the children, both of them boys, both unruly and both of them accident prone; every winter they would either break their heads while skating on the ice, or fall through it. She would threaten them with all sorts of dire punishments, her favourite being *ikh'l tsubrekhn dayne hent un fis gibn zey tsu dir oyf tsatskelekh* – I'll break off your arms and legs and give them to you as toys – though only Bashke could subdue them.

Our four homes stood a little apart from the rest of Barovke, and formed a sort of tiny 'suburb', though Barovke itself was a mere *shtetaleh*.

When I returned to Barovke in 1990 only one Jew was left, a tiny wrinkled figure with a bald head and hooked nose who looked like a tortoise that had been winkled out of its shell.

His name was Misha and he was an old soldier, indeed a hero of the Soviet Union, and had a large red star on his abode to prove it. He said he had lived in Barovke before the war.

I didn't remember him and he didn't remember me, which was hardly surprising, but I thought he might remember my father, Rabbi Azriel Bermant who, in Jewish terms, had been king of the place.

'Rabbis,' he said, 'rabbis? We had nothing to do with rabbis. They were fascist lackeys. My father was a communist. I am a communist. We were all communists.'

I was nine when I left Latvia, of an age to be aware of political expressions, even if I wasn't sure what they implied, but the Barovke Jewish community, as far as I could recall, was almost entirely composed of pious, God-fearing men. Some were more pious than others, and those who didn't fear God feared my father, but all kept kosher homes and one could expect to see them all in synagogue on Saturday morning – or nearly all.

There were four exceptions, Pinchashovitz the engineer; Heller the doctor; Hurwitz the dentist and Krochmal the apothecary, who were all part of the community in so far as they provided necessary services, but who otherwise kept their distance from it, and no one, not even father, expected them to do otherwise. They had come from large towns and studied in ancient universities, were members of respected professions, had steady incomes, lived in spacious homes and were in positions to make their own arrangement with the Almighty.

But communists? The word was on every tongue, but I presumed they had something to do with town life. I had never heard of them in a Barovke context. My parents may have been to blame.

My parents, in common with most of their contemporaries, did their best to shield us from unpleasant facts and whenever I asked a question about a painful subject – and a great many subjects seemed to be painful – they would answer, almost automatically, '*Du zolst nit visen fun dos, mein kind* – you shouldn't know of such things, my child.'

Communism and communists may possibly have been one of them. They were also reticent about the traumas they had suffered, and if they had any forebodings of the calamities ahead, they kept quiet about them. They were possibly right in believing that childhood was there to be enjoyed and that we would discover the harsh realities of life soon enough for ourselves.

My early childhood, certainly as viewed from Glasgow, verged on the idyllic. I had a close and affectionate family, an attractive mother, a highly respected father, a roof over my head, and boots on my feet. I rarely went hungry or cold, and the natives were friendly.

We had frequent visitors from Breslev, where my grandmother lived and which was just over the border in Poland, and they spoke of hatred, harassment, boycotts, beatings. One, a learned rabbi, showed a scarred chin where half his beard had been torn away. Another arrived swathed in bandages. 'Worse than Germany,' was the refrain, 'worse than Germany.'

There was nothing like that in Barovke. The Jews, in the main, were to be found in and around the centre of the village where they owned most of the shops, while the non-Jews were scattered among the surrounding farms. They lived separate lives, had different ways, and may have laughed at one another in private, but were otherwise on fairly good terms. Though again there were non-Jews and non-Jews.

Patushka, the Russian Orthodox priest who with his long beard and high fur hat looked like a Hasidic sage, used to spend long hours with my father bewailing the ways of the world. He could speak a bit of Yiddish and had even acquired Yiddish ways of expressing himself. 'You think you've got trouble with your Jews? You should only know of the trouble I have with my *goyim.*'

On the other hand there was a Lutheran pastor, a thin, austere, tight-lipped figure with rimless glasses with whom father rarely exchanged a word, but then he was Latvian and Latvian Gentiles were generally regarded as less friendly than the Russian ones. The friendliest *goy* of all was our Latvian neighbour, Jan, the village policeman.

The regime was spoken of – in whispers – as anti-Semitic, but no regime in eastern Europe was ever spoken of as anything less. I knew of several people who were said to be anti-Semites, but cannot recall a single anti-Semitic incident. I have fond memories of every Latvian I knew. I certainly have the fondest memories of Latvia as a place. I lived the life of Huckleberry Finn, fishing in the streams, swimming in the lakes, playing in the woods, running in the meadows under the great, open east European skies, and when we finally left for Scotland I felt as if I had been expelled from paradise ...

And yet when I look at myself in family photographs I see a skeletal, dark-eyed, dark-skinned, miserable little wretch. Nor do the adults around me, grandmother, uncles, cousins, aunts, look particularly happy; there is not a smiling face among them.

The cause may have been technical. These were not snapshots but professional photographs taken by a harassed and excitable professional photographer (who, to judge from the end product, could not have been all that professional), and by the time he had arranged the benches and bullied us all into place, we may have not been in a mood to smile. Yet there is all the difference in the world between a glum face and a wretched one, and I looked on the brink of tears, as if harbouring some private grief. And I was. I yearned for company, but was virtually friendless and while loneliness is always an affliction it is never as painful as in childhood.

I had three siblings, all girls. One was a few years younger than me, a babe in arms, and then a toddler, but always a nuisance. The others were several years older and seemed to belong to mother's generation rather than mine. They treated me with great, perhaps excessive, tenderness and affection so that I sometimes felt as if I had three mothers. I yearned to get away from the company of females and be a boy among boys, one of the gang, but was somehow kept distant.

The gang consisted of about 20 boys aged from six to eight and the leader was Zamke Zussman. I couldn't quite understand the reasons for his prominence, because young and small as we were, we had a keen sense of *yikhes*, pedigree, which goes with being Jewish.

To be a somebody among the boys, one's father had to be a somebody among men, and Zamke's father Shloime was a nobody, a *balagoleh*, a carter, which was about the lowliest calling open to Jews, a gruff, burly figure with thick lips, permanent bristle on his face, a belt of binding twine round his middle, and a whip in his hand.

Zamke may have been older than the other boys, was a little taller and wore long trousers while the rest of us wore shorts. He was lean, with rabbit's teeth and no eyebrows, and with his red cheeks and fair hair he didn't even look Jewish. He could, however, climb higher, run faster, shout louder and hit harder than the rest of us, and was the nearest thing among my contemporaries to a bully, and I suppose it was all a matter of sheer physical dominance.

Shaike Trupin, the second in command, was as frail as Zamke was robust and succumbed to every ailment going, chickenpox, whooping cough, measles, fever, scarlet fever, pneumonia. Dr Heller was in and out of his house. He was the one boy in Barovke with a room of his own, and it smelt of ether. He smelt faintly of ether himself, while the rest of us smelt strongly of sweat, garlic and *shmaltz* – at least in the winter, when we wore four or five layers of clothing. (Besides which there was no running water in Barovke so that we didn't wash all that often, or all that thoroughly, summer or winter.)

His frailty may even have added to his standing, for it suggested delicacy and breeding. He was also good looking, had his mother's blue eyes and, while the rest of us were regularly cropped, his hair was comparatively long. When I began collecting stamps and acquired a Greek stamp with a portrait of Lord Byron, he reminded me instantly of Shaike. He looked a prince and was of princely stock.

For a start his mother Soreleh was a *gerusha*, a divorcee, and Shaike's father, Shmuel Trupin, was her second husband.

I wasn't sure what the word divorcee implied, but it certainly suggested rarity, and while our mothers, even when young – and they were young – looked harassed and matronly, she looked like what one would now call a dolly bird, a crumpet. Divorce, whatever it was, clearly did something for a woman.

Soreleh could not have been all that young for she had a daughter by her first husband who was friendly with my sisters. She had a rather neat figure with a good bosom and a small underchin and, while most mothers had their hair severely pulled back into a bun, her hair was short, with a dark lock flopping seductively over her eyes and, while all mothers were aproned – except on the Sabbath and festivals – she was smartly turned out even on weekdays. She looked good even in the winter and, while other mothers thumped around in *volikes* – clumsy, knee-length felt boots – she wore an elegant pair of leather ones.

Everything about Soreleh was beautiful, her shape, eyes, profile, manner, movements, even her pubic hair, a neat little black triangle looking as if it had been trimmed by a hairdresser – which perhaps it had. (How I became familiar with her pubic hair will be revealed in a later chapter.) And unlike all our mothers, she never raised her voice. In our eyes she was everything a woman should be. We were all in love with her and one of the reasons why we all crowded round Shaike was because we all yearned for a glimpse of his mother.

And as if all that wasn't enough he was the one boy among us with regular pocket money which he spent on sweets, and shared them with us, and a large collection of toys – soldiers, pistols, popguns and balloons – which he didn't even have to share with his younger siblings.

His father Shmuel, a large, genial, portly figure, was a butcher, which in itself didn't mean much. He was, however, a prosperous butcher for he not only sold meat but made *wursht* – though there was speculation as to what actually went into his *wursht* – and money, even in Barovke, was a form of pedigree in its own right, especially as he also happened to be generous.

He was said to be a *goldener mentsh mit a goldenem harts* – a golden man with a heart of gold – but the most golden thing about him was his smile, like a burst of sunshine, for he had an impressive array of gold teeth and I should imagine that Hurwitz the dentist must also have been something of a goldsmith. It may even have been his main source of income, because one otherwise went to the dentist only for extractions. There were any number of toothless people about, but there was no one with dentures.

I believed gold teeth were a form of display, the only form open to men and that a man might have gold teeth as a woman might have gold earrings, though there were women – like my mother for example – who had gold teeth and gold earrings. (She presumably acquired both before she married, for father's income would never have run to such luxuries.)

Number three in the gang was Leipkaleh. He was short, squat, neckless and asthmatic with two bright, shifty little eyes. His father, Yossel, was an impoverished shoemaker, his mother was feeble-minded and he owed his position purely to his own merits. Learning also counted for something among us and he was widely held to be a genius and, while the rest of us struggled to master normal Hebrew letters, he was already familiar with the tiny script of the Biblical commentaries. He could read Russian, Latvian and German and could flesh out the stray names which kept cropping up in adult conversation – Mussolini, Hitler, Stalin, Jabotinsky, Pilsudski – with important details. Mussolini was bad, but harmless where Jews were concerned. Hitler was bad, and very bad for the Jews. Stalin was good, and good for the Jews. Jabotinsky was great. He couldn't make his mind up about Pilsudski, but in any case he was no longer in power.

There was a bloodless revolution in Latvia in May 1934 and we first heard of it from Leipkaleh who said that Latvia was now 'a fascist dictatorship'. I had no idea what the words meant – I'm not sure if he did – but he lowered his voice as he uttered them, and warned us not to repeat them or we would land in jail. 'There are spies everywhere,' he would warn us.

He was father's prize pupil, and I sometimes wearied of the praise he heaped upon him. 'He'll be a *godel hador*,' he would say, one of the great sages of his generation, and he planned to raise money to send Leipkaleh on to one of the great Lithuanian Talmudic academies, but a local philanthropist, Boruch Sholem, got in first and paid for him to be sent to school in Riga.

I tried to make inquiries about him when I returned to Latvia in 1990 which wasn't easy because I couldn't remember if his surname was Mossinsohn or Moisevitch, or even Moscovitch, and in any case he could have Latvianized his name, but I was told about a *zhidok* – a small Jew – from Barovke who had survived the war, had become a senior Communist Party Official in Riga, and had then vanished. It could have been Leipkaleh, and if it was, I suspect he is still alive, probably in Israel.

I can only remember three of the rest, Lazar, Welfke and Shmulik.

Lazar himself was eminently forgettable but he was part of a memorable clan. His father was known as Chatzkal-with-the-six-sons, and he was one of them. (Chatzkal also had daughters, but they didn't count for the simple reason that, while sons were regarded as an asset, daughters were thought of as a liability.)

Welfke was known as *der vilder*, the wild 'un, which was how his long-suffering mother described him. He was not so much wild as a *shleimazel*, accident prone. If we climbed trees and anyone fell and cracked his head, it would be Welfke. He was tall for his age, white-skinned and carrot-haired and thus easily identifiable, and if we were caught doing something we shouldn't he was nearly always the one they actually apprehended. The punishment he received on the spot was as nothing to the punishment he received from his father, a large bearded man who worked in Shmuel Trupin's shop and who was known as the *fonye*, an expression used to describe brutal Russian peasants.

He was a fairly ignorant man, but deeply religious and he would decribe Welfke in the words of Deuteronomy as a *ben sorer u'moreh*, a stubborn and rebellious son. Were it not for father's intervention he might have killed the poor boy, as it was he would whack him almost daily with a broad leather belt. Welfke would display his weals proudly the next morning, like an old soldier displaying the scars of war.

Our escapades, as escapades go, were fairly innocent. It was mainly a matter of raiding orchards, a plum tree here, a pear tree there and, according to Leipkaleh, such raids were well within the law, or at least within Jewish law, or failing that, within Leipkaleh's law, for – again according to Leipkaleh – 'the earth is the Lord's and all the fullness thereof', and we were fully entitled to anything we could carry away.

We sometimes went beyond fruit trees and raided sunflower plantations for their seeds and once, while raiding a field of broad beans, Welfke caught his testicles on a rusty barbed-wire fence and was gravely ill for months. He recovered but was never the same boy again.

Shmulik was even more unfortunate. His father couldn't make a living and his mother was mad, and people wondered if it wasn't their poverty which induced her madness.

During the week before Rosh Hashonoh, the Jewish New Year, special services are held in synagogue at the crack of dawn, and early one morning as worshippers were moving through the swirling mists they were startled by the sight of a naked woman running across the village square. It was Shmulik's mother.

They locked her up for a while, but she was eventually allowed home and would sit around in a long black dress looking like a bedraggled version of Whistler's mother staring into space and saying nothing.

Father organized a collection on her behalf and she was sent, accompanied by a nurse, to a famous doctor in Riga, but he couldn't help her. Neither could the Rebbe of Aknist, a young man with long blonde side-curls who was said to be a miracle worker. He placed his hands on her head, shut his eyes, directed his face to heaven and uttered innumerable prayers, but again without effect.

Where people were physically ill they could count on sympathy and support. Where they were mentally ill, they could only count on pity, and sometimes not even that, for such disorders, as far as possible, were kept secret.

Shmulik – a thin, sallow-faced grimy youngster with a runny nose and smiling eyes – seemed to take it all in his stride, and as his father was half crippled, he and his sister – who couldn't have been more than ten – more or less kept house. We treated Shmulik as our own *mitzva*, our private good cause. If he straggled behind in our marches, we waited for him. When we shared out our spoils, he was given first pick.

If Shmulik was not sorry for himself we were sorry for him and wherever possible we arranged our excursions to fit in with any free time he had, and whenever Shaike was incapacitated – a not infrequent event – he would stand in for him as Zamke's number two.

As the son of the rabbi, I should have been the *capo di capi*, the top of the lot, but I was not even a fully integrated member of the rank and file and served as a *nochshlepper*, a hanger-on.

It was not as if anyone actually warned me off, but I was kept in the dark, with little knowledge of what was happening and where it would happen, until it was all over. This was not all that important in the winter when the days were short and brutally cold and the snows were so heavy that we were occasionally housebound for weeks on end, and even then I sometimes missed out on a snow fight here, a tobogganing race there.

In the summer, however, the marching season began. The gang would assemble in the courtyard of Shaike's house and, after being drilled for some time, would march off in a long column with Zamke at the head, followed by Shaike and Leipkaleh, and the rest in twos, with me – if I was there at all – at the tail. We even had a drummer among us and were equipped with paper hats and wooden swords, but I found it difficult to keep in step and to add to my misery, my hat kept coming undone.

When we reached our destination – usually the woods – we would divide into two and engage in battle.

I can't understand why we came to play at soldiers, of all things.

We had never seen any films of battle because we had never seen a film. We had certainly never seen any battles and our only knowledge of war came from the wars fought between Abraham and Chedorlaomer, Joshua and the Amalekites and the struggles between the Maccabees and the Greeks, and the martial tradition which had prevailed among Jews was extinct by the time we were born.

Our parents spoke in subdued voices of the First World War, the Russian Civil War, and the Russo-Polish war, but never as combatants. Father did claim to have served in the Red Army which we found difficult to believe, because though he had an erect bearing he was the most unsoldierly of men. Zamke claimed that his father was in the cavalry, presumably because he owned a horse, a scraggy, motheaten nag with protruding ribs like a washboard, but he never seemed to be sure whether he had fought for the Russians, the Germans or the Poles, and left us with the impression that it might have been all three.

There was one Jew in Barovke, Binyomin Rosin, a massive figure with a booming voice, bull-neck and a gleaming hairless dome, who had actually been a professional soldier and had served in the Tsarist army for 25 years and, because of his size, was known as the Cossack. His long service would have entitled him to a pension and other privileges, which were forfeited with the Russian Revolution. No one knew what he did for a living, but he seemed to live fairly comfortably, and it was rumoured that he was a police spy.

It was said that Dr Heller had served as an officer in the German army, presumably in the medical corps, but he wasn't really part of Jewish Barovke and, in retrospect, it is clear that we got our inspiration for our soldiering from the annual military parade on Tzitsego Mayo, Latvia's Independence Day on 15 May.

Latvia had only emerged from the northern mists as a national entity in 1918.

The three provinces of Kurland, Livonia and Latgale had been ruled at different times by different neighbours and Russia devoured them all in the course of the eighteenth century. German, however, remained the lingua franca in most parts of the country and round our way, the intelligentsia – what there was of it – spoke German, the Jews spoke Yiddish, the peasants spoke Russian and, as far as I could see, the only people who actually spoke Latvian were those whose livelihoods depended on it, teachers, the policeman, the postmaster and the like.

Once Latvia became independent in 1918, the government took urgent steps to Latvianize the country and to enhance the sense of national identity, and Tzitsego Mayo not only celebrated independence, but was an assertion of national pride.

It was the event of the year. Every house in Latvia was required to have a flag staff, and the Latvian flag – white and blood-red – flew from every roof in Barovke. Flags and bunting were also strung across the main street, and a reviewing stand and platform were erected in the cobbled square.

The parade was at noon but we began to line the route long before to get a good vantage point and we cheered as important-looking figures pulled up in important-looking cars and took their place on the platform. Then came the band, their instruments gleaming in the pale sun, loud, sonorous, with thumping drums, followed by foot-soldiers, a magnificent sight in their long greatcoats, marching as one, their knee-length boots clattering on the cobbles. And finally, as a climax, the cavalry on the trot, rifles on their back, sabres at their side, the horses snorting and well-groomed, while a diminutive figure in a braided cape took the salute.

There were similar ceremonies in every town and village in Latvia but at such times we felt that Barovke was the centre of the universe. It was a stirring occasion and our soldiering was no doubt an attempt to ape the parade. Zamke even gave the orders in Latvian, which was about the only Latvian we understood. We saluted, presented arms, stood easy, stood erect and revelled in the sense of camaraderie which such occasions induced.

I say 'we', but it was really they, for even if I was allowed to take part in the parades I somehow felt out of them.

I was distressed by my exclusion, and mystified. I had the finest pedigree. I was not as good-looking as Shaike, but far from ugly, and if my mother was not as pretty as his, she was very attractive. I was not in Leipkaleh's class as a scholar, but then nobody was, and I was fairly bright. I washed as frequently as everyone else (which was not all that frequently). I was prone to pick my nose, but so was everyone else, but otherwise had no repellent habits. What did they have against me?

I suspect I was the victim of my own eminence. Father, as rabbi, was God's rep, and they may have feared that as the rabbi's son I might be God's nark. We all came from kosher families, but some of us – and Leipkaleh especially – had non-kosher ideas and often broached non-kosher subjects, such as fornication. 'Everybody does it,' I once heard him say, 'young, old, men and women, everybody. They do it in their sleep.'

Father noticed that when he entered a room conversation often stopped, not because people were talking about him, but because they were discussing a subject which was thought to be unfit for holy ears. It may have been the same with me. I was cramping their style.

We also spent a lot of our time in synagogue and while the others were allowed to mill around freely at the back and exchange gossip and play games, I was required to sit up front by my father right beside the holy ark, so that I was not only physically isolated but carried an unwelcome aura of sanctity.

In 1937 father went ahead of us to Glasgow to earn enough money to bring the rest of us over, and everything changed overnight. I was no longer the rabbi's son, no longer the nark, and no longer had to sit by the ark. But more than that, I was now rich.

Father sent us five pounds sterling a month. There were people in Barovke, not many, who earned more, but they were never sure if they would continue to earn it and were thus not free to spend it, while our fivers – in black print on white paper like graduation diplomas – came regularly and without fail. I had regular pocket money like Shaike, and like Shaike, was able to buy sweets and to share them. Leipkaleh had by then moved to Riga, and I was made number three. I was happy at last, not only as one of the gang, but as one of the leaders. But then, just as I was beginning to glory in my status, the packers arrived and we prepared to move.

Happiness, I discovered rather early in life, was a fleeting experience.

Chapter 2

Breslev

My earliest memory is of my maternal grandfather walking downhill at a rapid pace. He was wearing shiny, knee-length leather boots and a heavy sheepskin coat – a *peltz*. His coat was open and it must have been very windy for he was bent almost double and his long, grey beard, and the skirt of his coat, were carried sideways by the wind.

I also have a memory of him sitting silent and solemn at table, hardly eating, staring into space. I do not recall that his face ever lit up at the sight of me, his first, and at that point, his only grandson, or that he was even aware of my existence. There must have been other people at the table, but I was aware only of him, his long beard, his lined face. He died a year or so later and could not have been more than 60.

I was three at the time, and had two older sisters, Miriam and Sonja (or Merke and Soinke), and a younger one, Leba (or Lupke).

Mother's name was Feiga or Feiga Tsipke in full, both of which meant bird. I noticed as I grew older that people often lived up to their names, but there were exceptions. I've never lived up to my full name of Chaim Yitzchok, which means life and laughter, while there was nothing bird-like or chirpy about mother, though she could be fairly lively ...

We never celebrated birthdays in my family, but then neither did anyone else. First of all the Jewish calendar was so crowded with festivals that there was little room for private celebrations except for circumcisions, *bar mitzvahs* and weddings, but apart from that, people – and that included children – saw nothing to celebrate, and a good deal to regret, in the mere passage of time. People didn't celebrate silver weddings or golden weddings either, for the same reason (though in the case of the latter few people lived long enough to do so in any case, and where they did they were far too decrepit to contemplate celebrations).

Moreover, years, except where there was a *bar mitzvahs* in prospect, were rarely mentioned not only out of delicacy but because a great many superstitions surrounded the matter, and where one mentioned someone's age at all one added quickly, *zol er lebn bizkn hunderf un tsuantsik* (may he live to be 120 – as if anyone would want to). As a result I have only a vague idea of how old my parents were, except that they were born about the turn of the century, and that mother was slightly older than father, which was another reason why she was coy about her age. My younger sister was two years my junior. That much I remember because I would never let her forget it. My older sisters have never confessed to their years, but they always treated me as a child and when we lived in Barovke I tended to think of them as adults even though they were both still at school.

My sisters recall me as a large, dark, placid infant. If I was given drink I drank; given food I ate, and put to bed I slept. I am told that I never cried and when I fell out of bed I slept quietly on the floor until I was roused the next morning. Apparently I spent much of my time playing contentedly in a large sandpit at the back of the house, oblivious to the world around me, and eating every insect which crossed my path. (I was said to have had a particular fondness for beetles and would crunch them as if I was cracking nuts.) Had I been born 30 years later I would no doubt have been hauled to a child psychologist as autistic.

I was slow to sit up, slow to stand up, slow to walk and slow to talk, though when I finally did acquire the power of speech I spoke at the double (which I still do), and was found to be incomprehensible (which I still am.)

According to one sister my first word was *tsig*, according to the other, it was *tsug*.

Tsug means train. There was a small railway station on the edge of Breslev and the sight of the train may have made a great impression on me, as it certainly did when I returned to Breslev at the age of eight.

Tsig means goat and, like many families, we had one tethered in the back garden as our milk supply. (We apparently had a cow before that, but it died.)

I remember a lullaby which mother used to sing to my younger sister:

> *Unter Lipkele's vigele*
> *Ligt a kleyninke tsigele ...*

'Under Lupke's little cradle lies a small goat' but, as sung by mother, *tzigaleh* sounded much like *tsugele* and I wondered how a train, no matter how small, could have got under a cradle.

Miriam and Sonja often complained that mother gave far more attention to me than to them, that they were brought up by nannies, while mother saw to me herself, but it is likely that by the time I was around she could no longer afford nannies. For my part I felt she gave far more attention to my younger sister Lupke than to me, and certainly more affection, but such feelings are commonplace and are probably the source of all sibling rivalry.

Much as mother loved me, and I loved her, I tended to associate her with stern reproof for, while I was never actually mischievous, I always seemed to be getting in her way, getting things wrong, doing things wrong and making myself a nuisance. In other words, I was a *shlimazl*, and weather permitting – or even if it didn't – I did my best to keep out of her sight. That, however, takes us beyond Breslev.

Sonja's earliest memory is of mother in a long, black velvet gown with an ornate bodice, in a large room, looking very stately and beautiful.

She is not sure if she actually witnessed the scene or dreamt it.

Her next memory is of being placed on a table by my parents and being asked whom she would rather live with. Again she thinks it may have been a dream. Dreams can, however, be more telling than reality and it suggests that their marriage may have been going through a shaky phase which, all things considered, was not surprising.

My paternal grandfather was a pedlar from Kreslavka, a small *shtetl* near Barovke. He had three sons, of whom the second was my father, and all three were raised in abject poverty.

'We never went hungry,' said father, 'because we always had bread, and we never went cold, because you could always pick up a few bits of wood from the forest, but we didn't always have shoes, or rather we did, but we had to take turns to wear them.'

Father never had a secular education so I have no idea where he had learned to read and write Russian. He spent his early years in *yeshiva*,* some of them in Ponevezh. Although Father never talked much about the past, possibly because it carried too many bitter memories, when he touched on his *yeshiva* days a warm glow came into his eyes, his voice would tail off, and he would gaze into space. They were probably the happiest days of his life.

A *yeshiva* (plural, *yeshivoth*) has been variously defined as a Talmudic academy, a theological seminary, a Jewish monastery, a Hebrew academy, a hermitage and a retreat. It was all of these things and more.

The aim of a *yeshiva* was not only to produce scholars and teachers but to shape their character and outlook and arm them with the moral strength to live in the modern world without being corroded by it. The one thing it did not instil was intellectual curiosity, if anything it discouraged it. I never saw my father handle a secular work in any language, and there were certainly none in his fairly extensive library. He loved what he knew and distrusted what he didn't, in the general belief that everything worth knowing was to be found in the Torah. He did read

---

* After the war the central *yeshivat*, such as Slobodka (Hebron) and Ponevezh, moved from eastern Europe to Israel where they were re-established. They are today, as they were then, major seats of Jewish learning.

newspapers, in several languages, but never escaped the influence of the *yeshiva* and never quite lived in the modern world, not even after we moved to Glasgow.

We used to have a photograph taken about 1920 in Ponevezh *yeshiva* of some 200 tiny, disembodied heads, most of them bearded and all of them in black hats. One of them was father but we could never tell which – I'm not sure if even he could – for they all looked alike.

Strangely enough when Rabbi Joseph Kahaneman, the head of Ponevezh, a princely figure with a long white beard, glowing features and tired blue eyes, visited Glasgow in 1955 he recognized father instantly and they embraced like lost brothers.

Father was ordained as a rabbi, and a year or two later was introduced to my mother. They made a handsome pair.

It was, of course, an arranged marriage, as most marriages were. My mother's parents were, by chance, both called Daets, but they were not related, and their name suggests that they both stemmed from Germany.

Grandma came from a long line of celebrated rabbis though with her high cheekbones and large grey eyes, she did not look remotely Jewish. She must have been a strikingly handsome woman in her youth, for she was still handsome even in her old age – or what I thought of as old age, though she was only in her fifties. She was deeply devout, prayed often and, unlike mother, covered her head with a scarf which she tied under her chin. She looked and was rather severe. I couldn't remember seeing her smile once during the nine months I was there, but then I gave her precious little to smile about.

Grandpa was of mercantile stock and was a flax and corn merchant, and a fairly prosperous one, which was just as well, for he had six children – two daughters and four sons – and supported most of them and their families.

When mother, who was the oldest of the six, married he bought her a house in Breslev and set father up as a textile merchant.

When I was sent to stay at the house in 1938 I was amazed at its size. It was as big as any two houses in Barovke, stood in a large garden, and was more solidly built. The lopsided nature of

Barovke houses – their sagging doors, sagging windows, sagging eaves – made them appear to be sinking into the ground, which I took to be normal for human habitations, whereas our Breslev house was so upright as to be almost defiant. Grandpa was either very generous to mother, or very glad to be shot of her. She must have been about 20 or even 21 by then, an old maid by the standards of the day. Grandma had married at 16.

I have an attractive photo of my parents with their first child in the early years of their marriage that conveys an image of father which does not remotely tally with anything I knew of him.

For a start, in the photo he was bareheaded. He also had a small Lenin beard, a collar and tie, well-cut suit and a gold watch and chain and his whole bearing suggested success and prosperity. I don't know if he actually ever sought them, but both were to elude him throughout his life.

Father, in so far as he was cut out for anything, was not cut out for business. While some are masters of the hard sell or the soft sell, father was a master of the non sell, or rather, the give away. Everybody was short of money so that the local economy existed on credit but father, conforming to a well-known Talmudic precept, was disposed to trust everybody unless he had cause to distrust them, and was promptly snowed under with bad debts.

Moreover, if the weather was pleasant and business was slack, as it often was in the summer, he would close shop and go for a walk in the woods. And if the weather was dreadful and the streets were empty he saw no cause to open the shop at all.

He had two cronies, Chaim Isaac and Gilliskofsky, both of whom I was to meet in later years. The first was the local wit, a bright-eyed jovial figure who, given his circumstances had little to be jovial about, for though he was good company he was not much good at anything else. The second was a lawyer who must have been about as successful in law as father was in business. One or another of them, and sometimes both, would stop by for a chat or a game of chess and a glass of tea and mother complained that he was running a clubhouse rather than a shop.

Father also kept a volume of the Talmud open on the counter, so that even at busy times he did not always have his mind on the buiness and, but for the fact that mother helped out from time to time, the shop would have collapsed in the first twelve months.

She could not help out often because she was frequently pregnant and – according to my sisters – were it not for her many miscarriages I would have had nine or ten siblings instead of three.

Father continued to trade for two or three years before the business finally expired, and it may have been at this point that his marriage nearly foundered.

Grandpa must have had some faith in him for he set him up again, this time in *galanterei*, the haberdashery trade, which he combined with a small private Heder – the Hebrew and religious classes that prepared boys for their *bar mitzvah*. One of the boys exposed himself to Sonja while father was out of the room. She immediately grabbed a knife and would have recircumcized him had he not fled. (My wife, faced with a similar situation some 40 years later, reacted in precisely the same way: women are instinctive circumcizers.)

The haberdashery shop also collapsed, as did the Heder. By then there were three children about with a fourth on the way.

Father, according to mother, was very philosophical about it all, while she nearly went out of her mind, which doesn't mean to say that he was always calm, but possibly because they were so frequent, he rarely got excited about material setbacks.

One of father's problems was that he was a true believer, and as a true believer he was confident that the Lord would provide and, if the Lord didn't his father-in-law would, but by then grandpa's largesse and patience had given out. Father trained to become a *shochet* (ritual slaughterer) and, as if to obliterate his mercantile past, he grew a long beard.

My sisters recall a song which mother used to sing at this time.

Even light-hearted Yiddish songs with happy sentiments are often sad in tone, as if it was unJewish to be cheerful, while the sad ones drip with *weltschmerz*. One has to know Yiddish to grasp the utter misery they conveyed, but they can sound fairly bleak even in translation:

The whole world is a black hole, and everything is void and
    empty.
The distance is short from the cradle to grave, and life is no
    more than a dream.
Have you pondered yet on the dark night? My limbs tremble
    as I think of it.
I am but a child, and the grave awaits me.

And the tune matched the words.

My poor mother was prone to self-pity but at this time she had
ample reason to be sorry for herself. Her second pregnancy was a
difficult one and shortly after Sonja was born she woke up to find
her right arm paralysed. Local doctors could do nothing for her
and she travelled first to Vilna and then to Warsaw for treatment,
but they couldn't help her either. The paralysis was presumably a
form of hysteria for while talking excitedly to friends one afternoon she found herself waving her arm.

A year or so later, Sonja was taken grievously ill and, when
orthodox medicine proved unavailing, father turned to what
might be called ultra-orthodox medicine. According to the
Talmud a change of name can mean a change of fortune, and
Sonja – or Sonja Rive, as she was known in full – was given two
new names, Chaye (meaning life) and Alte (meaning old), with
the prayer: 'Just as her name has been changed, so may the evil
decree be changed from justice to mercy, from death to life, from
illness to a complete recovery.'

One may laugh, but it worked.

Sonja grew into a beautiful infant and mother kept her half
hidden in blankets and shawls to avert the *ayin-hora* – the evil eye.

There was, however, no changing the evil decree which had
descended on father, for he found it difficult to scratch together a
livelihood even as a *shochet*. Other men in his position had turned,
in desperation, to the same calling and there were, to quote a
familiar Yiddish expression, *mer shokhtim vi hiner* – more
slaughterers than chickens – at least in Breslev. It was a literal case
of cut-throat competition and when he was offered a job in the
nearby *shtetaleh* of Barovke, he took it.

It was not an easy decision. My two older sisters were by then in a good Jewish day school in Breslev. (It was a secular school but as they were girls their religious education was considered of no importance.) There was no such school in Barovke. Mother was part of a large, close and extended family which enjoyed considerable standing in the town. We had no relatives at all in Barovke and, though it was only a few miles away, it meant a border crossing. Poland had strained relations with all her neighbours so that borders were often closed. And even when they were open it was not all that easy to obtain the necessary permits so that, near as Barovke was in geographical terms, it was distant in psychological ones. Or, as the Yiddish saying went, *nokh a melukhe, nokh a velt* – another kingdom, another world.

My oldest sister, Miriam was particularly distresed at the thought of moving. She was 11 or 12 by then, doing well at school, attractive, lively, well integrated into the life of Breslev, and with many friends, the belle of the ball.

As the first grandchild she was close to grandma and was boarded out with her during the frequent and lengthy occasions when mother was ill. She was also very close to mother's younger sister Leika, so close that when Leika married she went with her on her honeymoon. And thus as we were preparing to leave Breslev she made it known that she had every intention of staying put.

My parents pleaded with her, it didn't help. Grandma and Leika added their pleas, but she would not be moved, and it was only after the entire family gathered round her to explain the situation that she finally relented, and even then she kept returning to Breslev at every opportunity so that I saw less of her than my other sisters and a certain distance developed between us.

If a change of name meant a change of fortune so – again, according to the Talmud – did a change of place. It is not so much persecution which has made the Jews a nation of wanderers, as hope.

Father did not actually bless the day he came to Latvia, but he did bless the day he left Poland, and would not set foot there again.

Chapter 3

Cutthroat

Father may have had grave apprehensions about moving to Barovke but once he settled in he found many compensations. In Breslev he had been an adjunct of the family Daets, and a fairly helpless adjunct at that, a *nebekh*. In Barovke he was not only someone in his own right, but an important someone, and treated with great deference, though not with such deference as to be paid a decent, or even a regular salary. Rather, he was paid on a per-throat basis, a few kopeks for killing a chicken, more for a sheep or a goat and much more for a cow. He also picked up a few kopeks from teaching and giving private tuition to boys from the more prosperous families.

Being a public employee had its drawbacks. Children are given naturally to boasting about themselves and about the attainments of their parents and in Heder one day we found ourselves discussing *tsedoko*, charity.

'My father,' claimed one boy, 'is the most generous man in town, and gives money to the poor and the sick and every other charity.'

'My father is even more generous,' claimed another, 'and gives ... '

At which I naturally chirped in with, 'My father gives – ' and was immediately cut short by a third boy who said brusquely: 'Your father doesn't give, he takes,' which was presumably a piece of wisdom he had picked up from his parents.

I was not so much offended, as distressed. Every Saturday night father would sit down to do his accounts, and little though he earned he always put something by for charity, a tenth in a bad week, more in a good one.

No one begrudged a cobbler, or a tailor his earnings, but then cobblers and tailors set themselves up in business and are not appointed by a public board. There was also a vague feeling that if a man was paid for performing a religious duty, he was somehow benefiting from public largesse.

We were not among the poorest in Barovke, and were certainly not among the prosperous, but we were among the solvent, and some people obviously resented our solvency.

Father, nevertheless, liked Barovke and its surrounding countryside, he liked the people, and found the non-Jews affable and friendly. Unfortunately, he hated his work.

That my father, of all people, should have been a cutthroat of all things, was one of the harshest ironies of fate, for he was gentle, almost meek, though on the rare occasions when his patience snapped he could become explosive.

The Jewish laws of *shechiteh* derive from an obscure verse in Deuteronomy: 'Thou shalt kill of thy herd and of thy flock which the Lord hath given thee as I have commanded thee,' on which the rabbis have built a mighty mountain of by-laws. A *shochet* is not only required to be a pious Jew but a learned one, and piety and learning go ill with butchery. In fact the job is much worse than butchery. A butcher need only hack away at carcasses, the *shochet* has to cope with living beasts.

Rabbis claim that in so far as any form of slaughter can be humane, *Shkhite* is the most humane form possible, but if it is humane to the beast it is cruel to the *shochet*. Some *shochtim* can, and do, become calloused to their calling. Father never did.

He would comfort himself with the thought that he was after all performing a *mitzvah,* and a necessary one at that, and would offer up a prayer before turning to his gory task, but it was not comfort enough. He hated every minute of it and was eventually broken by it. In later years, however, he would remind us that he saved our lives by cutting throats, for it was as a *shochet* that he was offered a job in Glasgow shortly before the war and not as a rabbi. Had he been only a rabbi, or even a successful textile trader, we would have remained in eastern Europe and would have perished with the rest of our family in the Holocaust.

The Latvian *shtetl* of Kraslava (Kreslavka, as it was known in Russian), where my father's family lived, was situated on the banks of the Dvina, near the Russian and Polish borders.

The Dvina (or Daugava in Latvian), broad and fast-flowing, was, and is, the lifeline of Latvia, so that the very situation of Kreslavka made it a place of some importance. It was also served by the railway and was thus doubly in touch with the outside world and compared to Barovke it was something of a metropolis. In 1897 it had a population of about 8,000 of whom more than half were Jewish. It was a flourishing community with several Jewish schools, a rich cultural life and some very prosperous residents.

Then came the war and in 1915, as elsewhere in Latvia, the Jews were deported into the interior. When peace finally came, not many of them chose to return and, by 1930, its population had declined to about 4,000 of whom about 1,500 were Jews.

Father referred to his home town only occasionally and then as a *shtot* rather than *shtetl*, but then his memory went back to the prewar years, and he once let slip the opinion that it was *treyf* – *treyf* being the antithesis of kosher.

He never explained exactly what he meant by it, but it may have had something to do with the fact that, until 1914, it was the home of a flourishing pork-processing industry which specialized in the manufacture of hog bristle, and which was owned and largely manned by Jews. The industry did not survive the war, which was probably why Kreslavka went into decline.

Working conditions in the factories were harsh and there were frequent strikes, and a radical tradition developed among the Jews of Kreslavka which persisted long after the factories closed. The largest Jewish organization in the town was the Bund, the extreme

left-wing Jewish Workers' League, whom father dismissed as
Bolsheviks. The second largest was the ultra-orthodox Agudat
Yisrael party, of which my grandfather was a member.

Father often visited his family in Kreslavka, but never took me
with him, possibly because he feared that I might be greeted with
sights and sounds which could be injurious to my upbringing. My
paternal grandmother died long before I was born – my sister
Miriam is named after her – but my grandfather – a short man
with a long, white beard and a red smiling face – conformed in
every detail to my idea of Grandfather Frost, or Santa Claus. He
also had the disposition of Santa Claus for, though he rarely had
two kopeks to rub together, he would – much to father's
annoyance – shower us with sweets. He would set off every
morning with a pack on his back to sell various household goods
to woodsmen, charcoal burners and their families in the nearby
forests. He was a devout little man and would also carry some
sacred text with him to read along the way and to comfort him on
the not infrequent occasions when he returned from a journey
without a sale.

Peddling for an elderly man in the heart of a forest was in some
ways a hazardous occupation and when father moved to Glasgow
he sent him a monthly sum so that he could stay at home, but
grandpa insisted that he would have continued peddling even if he
had been a Rothschild, for he loved the walks in the forest. He had
remarried shortly after the loss of his first wife, and peddling may
also have been a good excuse to get away from his second wife,
whom I never met but who, by all accounts, was a large,
formidable and intimidating creature.

He was shot by the Germans in July 1941, together with his
wife and five grandchildren. A sixth, my cousin Miriam, survived
and fled to Russia.

Her father, Yeisef Ber, my father's older brother, represented my
first experience of bad news.

I was about seven at the time and noticed that my parents
hardly spoke to each other at table, as if they had quarrelled, and
that they didn't seem to have all that much to say to us either.
Father was white-faced and drawn, and I could hear his anxious

tread on the creaking floorboards last thing at night as I tried to settle down to sleep.

Then came the telegram. I didn't know what a telegram actually was, but I was already aware that it meant bad news. My parents instantly vanished and it was my sisters who told me that uncle Yeisef Ber had died, and that my parents had gone to his funeral.

Yeisef Ber was taller than my father, with a slight stoop, very good looking in a sinister way and would have made an excellent villain in a grand guignol film. Like father he was a *shochet* and, like father, he hated his work, but father managed to survive to 64. Yeisef Ber died of cancer at 38. My parents had never mentioned his illness or his death. *Du zolst nit visn fun dos, mayn kind.*

My father had a younger brother with large glasses and a wild stare who lived in *shtetl* called Aknist. He married a wealthy woman whom he could never persuade to visit a place as humble as Barovke, and I remember him for three things. The first was his wild stare. The second was that he bought each of us large bars of English chocolate and I displayed my knowledge of reading by enunciating the word Cadbury's. And finally he arrived bare headed. To be sure he donned a *yarmulke* once he entered our house, but I associated bare heads with lawyers, doctors, dentists and he was a mere shopkeeper; nevertheless he was kindly and genial, if rather eccentric. I generally associated warmth with my father's side of the family, and money with my mother's side. He alone had both.

I have not been able to establish what happened to him, but as far as I know he did not survive the war.

I have trouble with names, or rather surnames, possibly because to Jews in eastern Europe they were comparatively new. Even in my time people were often known as the sons of their fathers or daughters of their mothers, or by their calling, their physical characteristics, or even deformities. Professional men, however, possibly because of their very standing, were always known by their surnames, with their professions as a prefix – Doctor Heller, Advocate Pinchashowits, Dentist Hurwitz, and Apothecary Krochmal.

On the other hand my father – whose full name was Azriel

Boruch Bermant – was never known as Rabbi Bermant but was universally referred to by the honorific Reb Azriel and I was not fully aware of what my own surname was until I was enrolled at school at the age of six.

My first memory of father was not a happy one. I was, as I have explained, a slow developer, late to sit up, late to talk, late to walk and, possibly because I was the only boy in the family, father was delegated to look after me, and one dark morning as he was helping me on with my boots, he threw a boot aside and growled, 'It's about time you learned to dress yourself.'

I was about four and the incident possibly lodged in my memory because it was the first time I had seen father show any sign of irascibility, as distinct from mother who could be – perhaps with good cause – irascible all the time.

Children take their cue from adults and I had great reverence for father because everyone else had. People rose when he entered a room. He had a natural dignity and looked tall because most people around him were short, and was slim, while most of the men around him were bulky.

Slobodka Yeshiva, unusually for such establishments, insisted that its students pay attention to their personal appearance and dress neatly, which was not easy if one had only one pair of trousers, as was the case with father, who sometimes had to borrow a pair for Shabbat.

By the time he moved to Barovke his beard – the colour of dried blood – had grown down to his chest. He never trimmed it while in Latvia but combed it frequently, and trimmed his moustache every Friday afternoon because a shaggy moustache could mean soup-stained lapels.

He must have spent a lot on clothes for, on the Sabbath and festivals at least, he was immaculately dressed. He had three jackets, or rather frock-coats, all with long vents at the back, which reached to below his knees – a grey one for weekdays, a black one for the Sabbath, and a black one with satin lapels for special occasions like Rosh Hashonoh and Yom Kippur. They were all made by our neighbour Chaim Ratz.

Father's shirts were handmade by mother, though on special

occasions he wore what he called his 'English' shirt, a pleated white creation, possibly a dress shirt, with a detachable collar and innumerable studs. I can't remember if he wore a tie, but it wouldn't have been visible if he did.

He would spend Friday afternoon preparing himself for the Sabbath, first by a visit to the bath-house, then by ironing his trousers, and finally by polishing his boots and paring his nails (and mine).

The iron, large, heavy and filled with glowing embers from the oven, was a terrifying affair, and I was equally nervous of the knife he used for his nails – and mine.

Knives were, of course, the tools of his trade and they varied in size with the size of the animals, small ones for poultry, bigger ones for sheep, and huge ones, almost the length of a sword, for cattle, though none of them was pointed or even rounded. They were all of stainless steel, and razor sharp. Father honed them daily and tested the edge with his nails. A notch, no matter how tiny, rendered them unfit for Shechita, and father adapted them instead for domestic use, the longest ones as bread knives, the shorter ones for slicing meat, poultry and vegetables, the shortest ones for nails. I was nervous of all three because one slip and you could lose a finger, and though father was fairly dextrous his fingers were often in bandages.

He was rather less immaculate on weekdays and would sometimes return from the abattoir speckled with gore, his beard caked with blood and mother always had the samovar on steam so that he could wash himself down.

He had an erect, almost soldierly bearing which was unusual among rabbis and, as I have said, he claimed to have served in the Red Army.

Mother's grey eyes lit up with amusement whenever he made the claim but it was not impossible, for Slobodka Yeshiva was evacuated to Minsk in White Russia during the First World War, and then to Kremenchug in the Ukraine. There was heavy fighting in both areas during the Russian Civil War and though he was anything but Red in outlook or temperament, he was fairly docile and could have been pressganged into the Red Army. If so he must have been something of Soldier Schweik, only without the low cunning.

He had a large, heavy, military watch, which was his one memento of army life, but it had been issued by the Tsarist army and he bought it from a Russian soldier.

There were no public clocks in Barovke and precious few private ones and people would time the onset of the Sabbath and festivals from father's movements. He had a large, high-crowned black beaver hat, and a long black coat, and on Friday evenings when he set out for synagogue with his coat over his shoulders like a cloak, shops would close at his approach like flowers at the approach of darkness, candles would be lit and Barovke assumed its Sabbath peace.

Because father was born about 1900 when Latvia was still part of the Russian empire, but left to study in Lithuania when he was about 12, spent the war years in Russia and the post-war years in Poland. When he came to Barovke in 1932, he was – in common with a great many other Jews – deemed to be an alien, a fact which was to have major consequences both for him and for us.

One word dominated the endless discussions he had with mother on the subject – *papirn* – papers. He had numerous papers which almost came apart through repeated handling, with different stamps on them, Russian, Polish, Lithuanian, Latvian, none of which, singly or severally, gave him the right to permanent residence anywhere. It did not mean he was completely stateless, but neither was he – to coin an expression – stateful, and he was always nervous of crossing frontiers for fear that one or another of his papers might be impounded, and that he might not be allowed to cross back. I think he even needed papers to move freely within Latvia itself.

He burned them all when he received his British passport in 1949 and made a blessing over the ceremony: 'Blessed art thou O Lord our God King of the Universe, who hast kept us in life, and preserved us, and enabled us to reach this season.

'Now,' he said, brandishing his precious document, 'I am a *ben khorin,*' a free man, at liberty to go anywhere, and come back. But its pages remained untouched for he never in fact left the British Isles.

Father served Barovke and its surroundings, including a *dorf* called Tartak which, if approached through the forest, was about eight miles away, and he would walk there and back once a week to cut a few throats and give private tuition to one or two boys.

He loved long walks, even very long ones, where there was something to be done at the end of them or, as he would put it in Hebrew, where there was a *skhar-halikha*, a reward for the journey. He found walking for its own sake – unless it was a casual *spatsir* in the cool of the evening – wasteful. In later years when I joined the Glasgow Scouts and spent whole days hiking in the hills, he couldn't see the point of it all. *Me vert oysgematert umzist* – you're tiring yourself out for nothing.

It was in Glasgow too that I first came upon the Brothers Grimm. Their stories were often set in forests, which were full of hidden menaces, but forests had no terrors for us in Latvia, at least in the summer.

In the winter we sometimes heard wolves baying from their dark depths and Tolk, the border policeman, once actually shot a large grey, emaciated wolf.

We were warned against going to the forests alone even in the summer because if one strayed from the familiar paths one could easily get lost, but they offered refuge not only from the fierce heat but adult scrutiny. They teemed with squirrels – red ones – rabbits, foxes, stoats. We picked wild strawberries and mush-rooms. The ground was carpeted, and the air scented with pine needles and, on hot afternoons, we were half-intoxicated with the smell of resins.

The forests were also the basis of the local economy. There were two stone churches in Barovke, and two brick buildings, the post office and a watermill (both of them still standing – the latter sans the wheel). Everything else was built of timber, sometimes of solid logs, but more often of planks caulked with pitch. There were woodcutters, wood carvers, charcoal burners and pitch refiners and the largest local concern employed about a dozen men sawing logs into planks.

There were also any number of carpenters who made furniture to order. Later, when on a visit to Dvinsk I saw a bed in a shop, I presumed it was for the private use of the proprietor ...

The Jews of Barovke were nearly all shopkeepers or artisans, and all the main shops were grouped round three sides of the village square, the fourth side being open. The largest shop belonged to Boruch Sholem Leibowitz, the local Rothschild, a shortish figure with a neatly cropped beard, tanned features, smiling eyes and a generous disposition. He was a textile merchant who dealt in good quality material, including English *shtof*, meaning worsteds and tweeds, and was prosperous enough to employ two assistants. He had a spacious home with a spacious courtyard, could entertain twelve people to a meal and provide them all with matching pieces of cutlery and crockery. He also had his own private bath-house, a unique luxury, and if most homes were illuminated by solitary paraffin lamps, he had a whole chandelier, but he was no magnate; if he had been he would have moved to Dvinsk or Riga.

Few Jews had any sentimentality about living in the countryside. There was no back-to-the-land movement among them, except for those who were anxious to get back to the Holyland. The very expressions *shtetl* and *shtetaleh* suggested urban tastes and aspirations. If others yearned for a *rus in urbe*, the Jew liked to think he was in *urbe* even when he was in *rus* and regarded his *shtetl* or even his *shtetaleh* as a town in embryo.

Nor did Jews have any strong sentiments about their locality, because few of them had been around long enough in any one place to acquire them. They lived in one area rather than another because that's where their bread was buttered. If they knew of an accessible place with better prospects, they moved to it. Few, if any, Jews in Barovke over the age of 20 had actually been born there.

There were small towns in eastern Europe, like Radun, which attracted many Jews because they were the seat of a great saint or sage. The nearest thing to both in Barovke was my father and great as I thought he was, he wasn't that great, and while several families left Barovke after he moved, none was drawn to the place because he happened to be there.

To live in a *shtetaleh* like Barovke was almost a confession of failure. Small was not beautiful, for if one had any ability and drive, one made it to a *shtetl*, and where one had ability, drive and *mazel* – luck – one graduated to a *shtot* – preferably Riga. And even Riga did not represent the peak of human ambitions, for many a Jewish family which had prospered in Riga moved on to London, Johannesburg or New York.

Father, however, was satisfied with small things. His favourite Talmudic quotation was: *Eyze hu ashir, hasomeah bechelko* – who is a rich man? He who is satisfied with his lot. He was far from satisfied with his lot, for he would have preferred not to have to cut throats, but he made the best of it, for if nothing else it gave him ample time for teaching and study, and he had an attractive wife of good family, a son and three lovely daughters (though he would have preferred it the other way about). Also, uncommonly for a rabbi, he had a strong pagan streak and loved the surrounding countryside, the lakes, the forests, the meadows, and had he not been forced out of Barovke, he would have remained there till the end of his days. (And of ours.)

'Not a *heilike shtetl*,' was his verdict, 'but a *geshmake shtetl mit geshmake mentshn*.' Not a holy village, but a piquant village with piquant people. It also had its share of eccentric people, or normal people with eccentric names.

There was, for example, *Zlate mit di zutzkes*, a large, plain woman with a long white face and large teeth. She was the daughter of Binyomin Rosin the Cossack and wife of Yankele the barber, though they looked like brother and sister. She had acquired her odd name because she always wore kirby grips (*zutzkes*) and was the principal conduit of local gossip, much of which she obtained secondhand through her husband.

Then there was *Breyne mit di burikes*. *Burikes* are beetroot and I don't know whether she acquired the name because she dealt in them or because, with her puce complexion, she looked as if she lived on them.

But then we nearly all did for it was such a versatile food and whether taken as soup, a salad or a drink, hot or cold, it was always wholesome and delicious. Mother even made a refreshing drink called *botvinya* out of beetroot leaves.

There was also, as I have said, *Chatzkel-mit-di-zex-zin* –
Chatzkel-with-the-six-sons. He was previously known Chatzkel-
with-the-five-sons, and might have become known as Chatzkel-
with-the-seven-sons, or even eight, but for a succession of
daughters who broke his run of luck.

Chatzkel, hairless, moon-faced and portly, was a mysterious
figure. He was often away for long periods at a time so that there
was speculation as to how he came by his sons and daughters. No
one knew what kept him away but whatever it was it must have
been worth his while for, by Barovke standards, he lived rather
well. His wife, a small, bright-eyed chirpy woman, bought her
clothes in Dvinsk and his oldest son had a bicycle.

Few people were addressed by their surnames and were
generally referred to by the diminutive variations of their
forename, Meishke for Moishe, Arke for Aaron, Yankel or Yankeleh
for Yaacov, and so on, but there were some people of such obvious
dignity and standing that they were usually addressed by both their
forename and surname, and one of them was Moishe Tzeitlin.

Tzeitlin owned the Harrods of Barovke. Like most Barovke
shops, it was a general store, but a comparatively posh one. Other
shopkeepers stood around in their waistcoats and shirtsleeves, or
wore brown overalls. Tzeitlin, a dapper figure with a tiny pointed
beard, wore a collar and tie and, unless he was actually seeing to
a customer, was always seated in a wickerwork chair as if he was
posing for a portrait, with one leg crossed over the other,
displaying ornate socks in the summer, or a pair of spats in the
winter. Everyone polished their shoes for the Sabbath, his were
polished even on weekdays.

Tzeitlin had no sawdust on the floor and sold nothing smelly,
no salt herrings, no smoked fish, no pickled gherkins, not even the
large slabs of red carbolic soap used in every household. He did,
however, sell small bars of perfumed or 'French' soap. They were
probably made in Riga or Dvinsk, but French was the local word
for luxury, much as English was the word for quality. He also sold
English chocolate. One saw few customers in his shop even on
market days and I don't know if he was actually prosperous, but
he always looked it.

He had a plain daughter with thick glasses and lank hair who
was a member of the youth wing of the Latvian Fascist Party, and
three sons, handsome and erect young men, the youngest of
whom caused a certain amount of scandal when he was seen
diving out of a window in Soreleh Trupin's house just as her
husband was arriving. His older brother caused an even greater
scandal when he was seen to alight from a bus on the holy
Sabbath.

Such details inevitably reached father who tended to act on the
principle that if he hadn't seen something it didn't happen; he
sometimes even went out of his way not to look.

Archick Grossman also kept a general store, but it was the
antithesis of Zeitlin's – small, busy, messy and smelly – the dominant
smell coming from a huge barrel of salt herrings in the doorway. In
the summer, when the barrel was kept inside the shop – to keep flies
away – the smell was overpowering.

People shopped often because they had neither the money nor
the storage space to acquire any large quantity of goods at any one
time so that I was sent on errands to Archick every day, sometimes
twice a day, now for a pound of sugar, now for a pound of salt, a
packet of candles, a tin of mustard, a box of matches, a herring.

The place was always crowded, and there were goods on the
floor, the counter and the shelves, with imperishables like
galoshes, paraffin lamps, buckets, hot-water bottles and chamber
pots dangling from the ceiling. Archick, in shirtsleeves and braces,
would rush hither and thither with sweat dripping from his beard.
He was helped in his shop by his wife and daughter, both of them
portly and slow-moving, with broad patches of sweat round their
armpits and under their bosoms.

I was never entrusted with money and got everything on tick.
So, I presume, did everybody else for, in all my visits to Archick's,
I rarely saw actual cash changing hands and, as not everybody was
in a position to pay in full, or even to pay at all, Archick, for all the
frantic energies he put into his business, was not a rich man.

Chaim Ratz, our landlord, on the other hand, was spoken of as
a *gevir* – a plutocrat – but didn't look it.

He lived across the road from us, but to put it that way suggests

a spaciousness to which Barovke never aspired. Our roofs almost
touched and when he sneezed, we said *gezundheit*. He was an
irascible old man and we heard all the angry exchanges between
him and his wife Bashke, who also had a temper and gave as good
as she got.

Her constant refrain was: '*Vos vilst u fun mayne yorn?*' – what do
you want from my years? – to his requests for regular meals at
regular intervals, among other things.

Ratz was said to be a *karger*, a miser, which didn't mean that he
never parted with money. Being religious he gave his obligatory
tithe to charity, but not a kopek more, which was the Jewish
definition of a miser. But again nobody knew how much he
actually owned or what he was worth. Nobody knew what
anybody was worth, but everybody made it their business to
reckon out what it could be, for Barovke was a community of
mutual assessors.

Whatever Ratz was worth he lived no better than us. His house
was more spacious for it included his workshop, but he ate no
better, and dressed no better, though he did have a fur-lined
overcoat with an astrakhan collar, which he also used as a dressing
gown, and one could sometimes see him taking a stroll in his
gatkes (long johns), galoshes and his astrakhan-collared coat over
his shoulders, with a bowler hat on his head.

He was proud of his bowler, which must have come from
England because I never saw another like it till I came to Glasgow.
He always wore it on Yom Kippur. (To my eyes it looked like a
cooking utensil, a pocket cauldron.) Father, as I said, wore a high-
crowned beaver hat, but that was his badge of office, and several
people had light grey or light brown fedoras or homburgs which
they wore on important occasions, but the standard form of
summer headgear was the black cloth cap with a black visor,
decorated in some instances with a black cord. In winter everyone
wore fur hats which went over the ears, except Patushka, who
wore his fur hat summer and winter – or rather he wore it in the
winter and fanned himself with it in the summer.

There wasn't a bank in Barovke. If there had been I don't
suppose anyone would have trusted it and from what I could see

old Ratz kept his wealth in an array of old Fry's cocoa tins.

He was a good tailor and wore a waistcoat covered in chalk and studded with pins, like a pincushion. He had an apprentice, the fair-haired son of a local farmer, a boy of about 14, who was becoming Jewish by contagion, for he covered his head when he ate and made a blessing – albeit in Russian – over his bread, and spoke a fluent Yiddish.

Ratz had a contract to supply uniforms. A great many people in Latvia wore uniforms, not only soldiers and policemen, but firemen, postmen and public officials of every sort and his workshop was full of magnificent brass buttons. It couldn't have been a large contract, but he was the only local Jew to be so favoured by the authorities, even though he hardly spoke a word of Latvian.

His fortune, however, did not come from tailoring, for he owned several houses, including ours, and patches of farmland which he leased out to his neighbours, which is how we came to have a potato and cabbage patch.

He was very devout and one would see him in the early morning giving orders to his apprentices while still wearing his *tallis* and *tefillin* (prayer shawl and phylacteries), and would spend more time in praying before and after meals than on the meals themselves – possibly because prayers were less expensive than food.

He was one of my father's small retinue of *tsadikim* – saints – as father called them, with perhaps more than a touch of irony – who would meet with him in the main synagogue in the evening to study the Talmud.

Father's main joy in life, other than his children, was the Talmud, but Talmud study is a little like drinking. It is a convivial occupation, and calls for a *khevruso*, company, and father's *kheuruso* was a fairly mixed one and rather ancient.

Father himself was only in his thirties then but, possibly because of his long beard and grave demeanour, he always looked old to my eyes, and his *tsadikim*, apart from Ratz, included Archick, Moshe Yudeh, Shimshon Ber, Beirach Fleischman, Yossel the shoemaker, Mendel der geller, Mendel der schwartzer and, a little improbably, Binyomin Rosin the Cossack.

Rosin was semi-literate but he liked to move among learned men, possibly in the hope that some of their learning might rub off on him though, because of the rumour that he was a police spy, he might have joined the group in case anything subversive was being taught. He would, however, join the arguments in his loud, booming voice with gusto, even if he couldn't always understand what they were about.

Yossel the shoemaker was marginally more learned than Binyomin Rosin. He started coming to the Talmud group after father had pronounced his son Leipkaleh an *iluy*, a prodigy, and he obviously felt as the father of a prodigy he could do no less.

Moshe Yudeh was the synagogue beadle who taught the younger boys in the local *chedrum*, where he was known as *klapper*, or thumper, for he used to thump us on the back, not to keep order but to help us study. He seemed very old to me but could not have been more than 50. A lean, cadaverous figure, with sunken cheeks, he had a long face made longer by a straggly beard, a glum expression and a faint, plaintive voice, as if someone had him by the throat. I had never known him to smile once, but then any man who has to teach small boys for a livelihood has nothing to smile about. As beadle he also had to supervise local funerals, but that he found a comparatively congenial occupation and if his features never expressed anything like joy at such occasions, they did at least show passing signs of animation.

Shimshon Ber was the oldest man in Barovke, and looked it. (The oldest woman was a shrivelled, little, black-clad Russian *babushka*, bent double with age, with a wooden leg and a long nose who claimed to be 107 and was said to be a witch. We were all afraid of her and when we heard the thumping sound of her wooden leg we would run for cover.)

Shimshon Ber was said to be 100 but could not have been much more than 90 and was as cheerful as Moshe Yudeh was glum. He had a white beard which went down to his navel and was the one green-fingered Jew in Barovke. Everyone grew – or tried to grow – something, but it was always something edible.

Shimshon Ber found pleasure in growing mere flowers, delphiniums, roses, geraniums, dahlias, chrysanthemums, but he took particular pride in his sunflowers which towered several feet above him, and he would stand beaming among them like a species of sunflower himself. He had outlived most of his family and was looked after by a shrivelled, toothless, widowed daughter who looked older than him.

Beirach Fleischman, a tall, genial figure with a reddish beard, who had little to be genial about, was one of the two Jews in Barovke with a private phone. The other was owned by Pinchashowits the engineer, who was rich. Beirach had a phone because he was poor. It was his livelihood and if you were anxious to contact the outside world, or to be contacted by it, you went to Beirach's. You had to book such calls and paid whether you made them or received them.

His phone was an elaborate contraption built into the wall, with a cranking handle, and you had to shout to make yourself heard. Or rather it was believed that you had to shout so many decibels when talking to Dvinsk, a few more when talking to Riga but, when talking to New York you bawled at the top of your voice so that when you made or received a call at Beirach's the whole of Barovke knew about it; on warm evenings people would hang round the open windows of his house in the hope of overhearing an exchange.

The trouble was, one only heard one side of the conversation:

'He's what? ... Not coming? What d'you mean he's not coming, it's all arranged. My mother-in-law's coming from Dvinsk, my sister-in-law's coming from ... He's got what? ... Malaria? ... He thinks he's got malaria? ... Look, if he had malaria he'd know it, but in any case how did he get malaria in a place like Schwintzyan? ... Where? ... What was he doing there? ... Was he ... Did he? ... Has he? ... Did he bring anything back? ... Yes, but apart from the malaria ... Well, that's something ... But what'll I tell my poor Hanah? She'll be heartbroken ... Yes, but couldn't he wrap up warmly? Malaria never killed anyone ... Did he? ... Was he? ... I never knew ... Must have been a bad attack ... I'll tell her ... I'll tell her ... I don't know how she'll take it but I'll tell her.

Don't know how my wife'll take it either. Wish him a speedy recovery ... '

Father owed his standing in Barovke to his office, Boruch Sholem to his wealth, Shmuel Trupin to his generosity, Shimshon Ber to his antiquity and learning, Moishe Zeitlin to his dignity and style. Beirach had none of these things, yet was *gabai* – senior warden – of the main synagogue, and owed his standing to his very warmth, and his readiness to assume burdens from which others would flee, and one of the reasons why he may have found it difficult to make a living was that he devoted so much of his time to public service.

Another possible cause for his penury was the fact that he had many daughters. I can't in retrospect distinguish one from the other. They were all exceedingly attractive in much the same way, with high spirits, dark eyes, bright smiles and dimpled cheeks. They were all of marriageable age and all married well in rapid succession to prosperous businessmen in Dvinsk and Riga; and there seemed to be a wedding in Beirach's almost every other week.

Wedding guests from Dvinsk were substantially like people in Barovke, but they looked better dressed and better fed. Guests from Riga, however, looked as if they descended from another planet. They had soft felt hats, their jackets matched their trousers, they wore ties and they tended to speak German, or even Latvian, rather than Yiddish.

There were no written invitations to weddings. Moishe Yudeh would get up at the end of the Sabbath service, bang on the table to obtain silence and announce the time and date of the event. Everyone was invited, or at least everyone turned up, including all the small fry in the place. If there was a wedding in the evening people didn't have lunch.

Catering was a communal affair. Every housewife contributed, a cake, a dish, a bottle of wine, a number of glasses, a few chairs, and several items of cutlery and crockery. Mother's usual contribution was *pu'tchah*, also known as 'fish-noga' or calves'-foot jelly, with hard-boiled eggs and raw onion sliced into it, frozen hard in winter, slightly soggy in summer, but always delicious. The venue was usually the *pahzharne*, the local fire station, with a backdrop of drying hoses, and a constant smell of pitch.

Music was provided by Yankel the barber, who, of course, played the trumpet, a fiddler and a small man with a double bass who, at frantic moments, seemed to climb up and down his instrument like a performing monkey.

Beirach had a boy called Moishale, of about my age, with six toes on one of his feet. He always wore boots and stockings, even in the summer, when the rest of us ran around barefoot, not because he was embarrassed by his deformity but because it was his stock in trade. There were always visitors in the summer, and if they wanted to have a sight of his supernumerary toe he would charge them a caramel.

Mendel der geller and Mendel der schwartzer were so called because the one had a ginger beard (*geller*) and the other had a black one (*schwartzer*). And there was in fact a third Mendel in Barovke known as Mendel der krumer (the bent one – physically rather than figuratively).

Both the bearded Mendels were excitable even in the normal course of life and when they turned to the Talmud they could become explosive for Talmud study is a form of dialectic and is often an attempt to reconcile irreconcilable arguments.

It doesn't take much for two excited men to trigger off everyone else, and the Cossack would join in with his boom, Moshe Yudeh with his whine, Archick with his shriek, and Shimshon Ber, the most quiescent and gentle of men, would bang the table with his fist and roar at the top of his voice. Even father, with his mild disposition could become animated on such occasions and would flail his arms, raise his voice and wave his thumb. The building would quake with the tumult and on warm evenings, when the windows were open you might think someone was being murdered, and someone might have been, but for father's presence. He revelled in it all. A *gute shvure*, he would say, a good talking point. Where there was no passion there was no joy.

Chapter 4

Queen Mother

If father was king of Barovke, mother was queen, not because she happened to be the wife of the rabbi, but because she happened to be the woman she was. And if father, in the main, regarded his flock with affection, mother tended to regard them with disdain, not so much as individuals, but as a group.

She had a high regard for Boruch Sholem, she liked Shimshon Ber, she was fond – as everyone was – of Shmuel Trupin and had a soft spot for Moishe Zeitlin. There was, in fact, hardly anyone she actually disliked but she did not care for Barovke as a whole. It was small, poor and backward and was a constant reminder that she had come down in the world. Or rather, she was angry with fate, and vented her displeasure on Barovke. She was also angry with father, but that's another story.

Her attitude did not endear her to Barovke, and some referred to her mockingly as the Tsarina, but most people tolerated her airs and graces, not only out of respect for father, but because they took her at her own face value and believed that she added a touch of class to the place.

She was, or so we were given to understand, born into a prosperous family of high standing which was 'ruined in the Russian Revolution'.

Every Russian Jew with money – as well as quite a few without
– who survived the Revolution claimed to have been ruined by it.
I don't know how rich my grandparents actually were but they
retained relics of earlier prosperity, fine china, silver cutlery, silver
candlesticks, gold trinkets, a tendency to rely on servants. They
also looked vaguely aristocratic, especially grandma with her erect
bearing and imperious air, and people certainly deferred to her as
if she was a woman of some importance, or at least a woman of
means.

I last saw her in April 1938. She was 60 at most, a white-haired
old woman. I had by then spent nearly a year with her which may
have contributed to her rapid descent into old age. People –
certainly in eastern Europe – aged quickly, however, in those days
and a woman of 60 who could still get around under her own steam
felt she was doing all right, while a woman of 70 was regarded as
ancient. Anyone older than that was a freak. Longevity, where it
existed, never assumed the scale of an epidemic. And, if it comes
to that, longevity in eastern Europe isn't all that common even
now. When I returned to Barovke in 1990 I found very few people
around who were much more than 50.

In later years mother wondered how she had lived through
everything she had lived through with her sanity intact. She was
born about 1900 – I never knew her exact age – in what was then
Belorussia. Then came the war with all its chaos and in 1915, the
deportations.

The Russians, as I have said, questioned the loyalty of the Jews
in the western marches, but given the oppression and hardship
they had suffered under Russian rule, they had no cause to be
loyal.

Mother's family must have lived under German occupation at
some point of the war and even with the sound of guns echoing in
the distance, they experienced a period of stability and order they
had not previously known, but it was short lived. In 1917 came
the Revolution, followed by the Civil War which was
accompanied, and then followed by, the Russian–Polish and the
Polish–Lithuanian wars. The Poles, under the inspired leadership
of Pilsudski, emerged victorious on every front, and acquired

large tracts of Lithuania and Belorussia, which is how I happen to have a Polish birth certificate dated 26 February 1929. And which is why I have at various times and with varying degrees of accuracy been able to describe myself as Russian, Polish, Lithuanian and Latvian. It was only when I returned to my birthplace in 1990 that I discovered that I was actually Belorussian.

Mother's family was from Vitebsk. She never explained, and I never asked, how they came to end up in Breslev. Vitebsk was a *shtot*, Breslev was a *shtetl*, which was one comedown. Barovke was a *shtetaleh*, which was another, and she never quite reconciled herself to it.

For a religious Jewish woman of her time she was uncommonly well educated, for she could read and write in Yiddish, Russian and German and knew more than a smattering of Polish and Hebrew.

Orthodox Jews put the highest stress on education and regarded it as the greatest good, but only where sons were concerned, and they were sometimes nervous of giving their daughters an education at all.

When my sister Miriam won a scholarship to the Dvinsk gymnasia at the age of 12, father was proud of her achievement, but troubled by it.

'*Vos darf zi dos?*' he asked mother, what does she need it for? He feared that a good education could impair her desire to settle down and damage her marriage prospects.

In mother's generation, certainly, many women were illiterate, and when she was a girl it was customary for some synagogues to employ *forzogers* – foresayers – in the ladies' gallery who would read out prayers line by line, which were then passed along the row in a succession of Chinese whispers and the most sacred phrases from the liturgy would sound like blasphemy by the time they reached their final destination.

Mother's formal education came to an end with the outbreak of war in 1914 and she claims that she picked up what she knew from her four brothers, who had a succession of private tutors and who were fairly learned.

Mother seemed to have been familiar with the works of Tolstoy, Dostoevsky and Pushkin, and all the Yiddish classics but must have acquired her knowledge in her younger years for I rarely saw her with a book in hand but then, given the demands on her time and the state of her health, she rarely had an opportunity to read.

She did not appear to have many friends in Barovke and the nearest thing she had to a confidante was Titania, the wife of Jan, the village policeman.

Titania was so large and blonde as to make mother seem slight and swarthy, but both stemmed from large towns, both were comparatively well educated, both believed they had come down in the world, and both felt that they were married to good, kind, but ineffectual men.

Jan was a lean, spare figure with a quiet voice and retiring manner who was totally devoid of the officiousness one expected of a man in uniform, especially with a gun in his holster, but then Barovke was a fairly orderly place. A drunk might go berserk from time to time and strangle his wife or murder his neighbour, and there were instances of petty theft but there was otherwise hardly any crime in the neighbourhood. One did, however, need permits for almost everything, especially if one was not a Latvian citizen – which was the case with many people in Barovke – and he spent much of his time examining documents and stamping papers.

He was Latvian – he would not have got his job otherwise – and his wife spoke of him dismissively in his presence as a peasant.

Being a woman of delicate susceptibilities she was of delicate health, as was mother, though unlike mother she did not look it but her blooming exterior covered a multitude of chronic disorders.

Mother was prone to fainting fits which alarmed us all, and especially me, for she turned a deathly white and every time she passed out I thought she was gone for good.

My sisters later – much later – told me that mother's tendency to pass out was due to her frequent miscarriages, but she was also prone to other disorders.

In Barovke medicine – or at least orthodox medicine – was not taken lightly, or at all if one could help it, for it was expensive, and for minor maladies one resorted to old wives' remedies, dock leaves for cuts, butter for burns, a *gogel-mogel* – the yellow of an egg with sugar whipped into boiled milk – for bronchial disorders, and hot and cold compresses for almost everything else. Where they failed one turned to *bankes*, which in Barovke were administered by Nehama die Boderke.

Nehama, a large-faced woman with bulging eyes, was the local bath attendant (hence die Boderke), but *bankes* were possibly her main source of income for she would be called out to apply them at all times of the day and most hours of the night.

Bankes were glass cups like tiny pudding basins, which she would heat with a burning piece of cottonwool. The flame would consume the air in the cup and cause a vacuum, and she would then immediately screw it into the back of her patient, or victim, throwing all her great weight into the effort. She would use about a dozen cups at a time, and the sight of a prostrate figure with a dozen cups in his back like great glass carbuncles could be rather startling as, indeed, was Nehama herself with her rolled-up sleeves, her sweating brows and heavy breathing.

It may sound crude, and certainly looked crude, if not alarming, but it often worked and was used for aches, pains, fever, bronchitis, catarrh, flu and a host of other maladies, major and minor, and Nehama would point out that even if she couldn't cure everybody, she never actually killed anybody, which was more than could be said for orthodox medicine.

Where Nehama's efforts proved unavailing one went round to Krochmal, the apothecary, to see if he had any helpful suggestions.

Krochmal was a portly figure with rimless glasses, bristle growing out of his nose, soft hands, and a crisp white coat whose buttons didn't quite meet – or met with difficulty – and he smelt of ether and sulphur. He had a stained-glass window in his place which sent a blue glow over him and everything about him, and which made him look and sound rather eerie. He was always helpful and whatever the ailment he had something to recommend, which he would make up on the spot with mortar and pestle and package in a small piece of white paper known as a *proshik*.

In earlier days one also had *felshers*, licensed but unqualified medical practitioners who were allowed to deal with small injuries and minor ailments. To summon an actual doctor, however, one had to be seriously rich or seriously ill. And he was almost invariably summoned because if one was well enough to make it to his surgery, one was well enough to manage without him.

Our local physician, Dr Heller, was a short, slight, bald-headed man, who must have been familiar with Yiddish, but preferred to address his patients in German. Had he done so in Yiddish, doubts might have arisen about his competence, for if English meant quality, and French luxury, German was the language of proficiency.

Heller was the only man in Barovke to own a pair of pyjamas, or at least the only one to wear them in public, though not when making house calls. We did not think of them as nightwear, for we slept naked in the summer, and in our underwear in the winter, but presumed that pyjamas were something which a man of fashion might wear on a warm summer's day. (When I got my first pair of pyjamas in Glasgow, I wore my pyjama jacket to school.)

Heller didn't have a car and went everywhere on foot, black leather case in hand, under his own cloud of ether.

He was a frequent caller and I have vivid memories of the urgent preparations made for his visits. Rooms were tidied, beds were made, floors were scrubbed, and we would all approach him with the greatest deference, as if he was a being from a superior universe – which to our eyes he was.

Good health was the ultimate blessing, and bad health the ultimate curse. When you were angry with somebody you didn't tell him to go to hell, you wished him a bout of cholera (*A choleriyah af dir*). When men would talk in hushed voices of this setback or that misfortune, they would often comfort themselves with the refrain, *abi gezunt* – meaning as long as you're healthy nothing else counts.

Gezunt – health – was, and is, about the most frequently used word in the Yiddish language, and was uttered with every breath; *zai gezunt* – stay healthy; *gei gezunt* – go in health and, of course, *gesundheit* – you should be healthy.

In the circumstances the doctor enjoyed an even more exalted status than the rabbi. The latter merely assured your wellbeing in the hereafter, the former was concerned with the here and now. Where his intervention failed, as it often did – if only because a patient had to be on the brink of death before a doctor was summoned – it was treated as an act of God, but where the patient actually recovered the name of the doctor was trumpeted abroad as a miracle worker.

Heller expected to be paid on the spot which, all things considered, was a necessary precaution, though I suspect that father – being, so to speak, in the healing trade himself – got special terms.

My parents rarely spoke of health problems in front of us children, Mother and Titania rarely spoke about anything else. I, of course, wasn't supposed to listen or, as they spoke in Russian, I was not supposed to understand, but many Yiddish words are of Russian origin and one didn't have to know much Russian to grasp the meaning of *aperatziya*, though expressions like *geeneekolhak* or *kheerork* were lost on me ...

Both mother and her friend were, as I said, of delicate health – which was possibly one of the reasons for their friendship – and it went with their status as ladies of good breeding, for if a healthy body was the ultimate good, brutish good health suggested a want of refinement.

There were no specialists in Barovke, and there was no hospital. If one was referred to a *kheerork* or a *geeneekolhak*, or if one needed an *aperatziya*, one took a bus to Dvinsk. Mother went to Dvinsk for such purposes on a number of occasions and was sometimes accompanied by father. At such time we were left in the charge of Raizel, wife of Moishe Yudeh, the *shammos*, or beadle of Barovke.

A beadle in English civic lore was a person of some authority and standing. The *shammos*, in Barovke at least, was the lowliest public servant, though in larger communities they had someone even lowlier, known as the *pots-shames*.

Every *shtetl* had its quota of *nebbichs*, but the *shames* was a *nebbich* by the very nature of his calling, and Moishe Yudeh was everybody's dogsbody. Poorly housed, poorly paid and poorly treated, he augmented his tiny income with a variety of odd jobs, mainly in teaching, while his wife Raizel did a bit of cleaning for this family, a bit of cooking for that and was known as a *kvaktuche*. The word is onomatopaeic, and means a plaintive, brooding hen. She was a short, stocky woman, with small, bright eyes, a large bosom before her and a large bottom behind, and it was her rueful, raucous squawk which announced her presence.

I don't know how she got her portly shape for she never seemed to eat, and rarely stopped working.

She certainly never stopped talking, not so much by way of conversation, but by way of complaints and imprecations addressed to God in Heaven and the world at large.

She cursed her parents for bringing her into this world, her husband for being useless, her daughter for being feckless, and the people of Barovke for being thieves, scoundrels and cutthroats – *ganovim, gazlonim, ratskhonim*. The only person she spoke well of was father, 'a *guter yid*, a *fayner yid*, an *eydeler yid*, a *tsadik* – a good Jew, a fine Jew, a gentle Jew, a saint. Without him, she would add, Barovke would be worse than Sodom.

If one inquired after her health – as one does by way of greeting in Yiddish – she would reply 'don't ask', and then go on to describe the disorders in every organ in her body. One day she would complain of stones, another of sugar, a third of water, and sometimes all three. A medical student trapped in her company for a day would, if he survived it, pass his pathology exams with flying colours.

Mother's ailments would cast a shadow over the entire household, for even when she was not so ill as to require medical attention, we would have to walk softly – not easy on wooden floors with creaking floorboards – and talk softly in case we might disturb her. She often lost her voice and would ping her glass with a teaspoon if she wanted attention. We would sit with ears cocked for her pings, and if ten minutes passed without one, we would tiptoe round to her room to see if she was all right. But perhaps even worse than her ailments was the thought of having Raizel among us.

Father would never let us utter a harsh word against her, and insisted that the woman was a *tsidkones*, a saint, for she was always ready to help anyone in difficulties. She may not have done so cheerfully, or uncomplainingly, but did it unstintingly.

Mother had a daily – or was it weekly? – help in the person of Anna, a bosomy Russian woman and a heavy smoker. She used old newspapers to roll her own cigarettes. They burned like a flare and filled the house with a smoky mist while she was around. Mother often complained about her but could not have done without her. I was fond of Anna and Anna was fond of me. She would clasp me to her bosom every time she came and I was half suffocated by the smell of tobacco and sweat.

My sisters told me that I had a Russian wet-nurse, a huge woman who would sit swaying and singing Russian songs with me at her breast. What with my wet-nurse and Anna I acquired an obsession with bosoms – and a love for Russians – which I have not yet outgrown.

I could understand a bit of Russian but found Anna totally incomprehensible, partly because she always spoke with a cigarette in her mouth, and partly because she used the local dialect.

Anna had a friend called Dumiche, a large grey-haired woman with one brown tooth in her mouth, and a loud, ribald laugh. She was a bricklayer by profession and smoked a pipe. After work she and Anna would often sit together in our garden, and when they both lit up they sent up a cloud which sent birds flying from the treetops and half obscured the sun.

People often spoke of poverty in Barovke but I never discovered the full meaning of the word until Anna took me to her house, a wooden cabin in the forest hardly bigger than a garden shed. Her husband – or the man I took to be her husband – was a charcoal burner. There was a broken down-chair, a wobbly table with a few crusts of bread, a few bare shelves against the wall, and a bundle of rags in a corner by way of a bed, but Anna made a drink out of old bread called *kvasch*, which tasted heavenly to me.

On the rare occasions when she was in good health, mother could be very industrious and would apply herself with great vigour when it came to sewing, cutting, stitching, knitting and baking, but – except on the approaches to the Sabbath and festivals – she had little patience for other domestic chores. Anna would do the laundry and scrub the floors, and we had a small book-lined room where father received visitors and which was always kept tidy, but otherwise beds remained unmade, floors unswept, furniture undusted, tables uncleared and cutlery and crockery unwashed. One of the reasons why I looked forward to the Sabbath and festivals was that they were about the only occasions when the house was tidy.

Father, though tidy in person, was untidy in habit. He would leave half-eaten apples and half-smoked cigarettes all over the place and would scatter ash wherever he went. I suspect that the trouble arose out of the fact that men in most Jewish households were never required to lift a finger around the house in the general belief that they were ordained for higher things. I was certainly never expected to help out at home and only learned to make my own bed after I joined the Scouts, and the mess I recall may have been due less to mother's laziness than our slovenliness.

In fact laziness was hardly the issue and I suspect that mother's disinclination to cope with domestic chores arose out of her belief that she too was intended for better things.

It was also not all that easy to keep homes, or even one's person, all that clean because water was fairly expensive. We were surrounded by it on every side, lakes, ponds, rivers, streams, but none of it was on tap. As there wasn't even a parish pump, water was obtained from the village well and bought by the bucket from a dusky gypsy woman who functioned as the village water-carrier; when one has to buy water by the bucket one uses it sparingly.

If mother was unhappy with her lot, father was certainly unhappy with his and my sisters believe that they were unhappy with each other. For a start mother was a bit older than father, which in their eyes was a sign of desperation. She was attractive, shapely and spirited and could be amusing, while father was bookish and retiring and, compared to her, he verged on the inert. She was also of 'good' – meaning monied – family, which father manifestly was not. My sisters once asked her why she married him, and she said: 'There was a war on, men were scarce. He was good-looking, learned and had a good name and I took what I could get.'

Father overheard the exchange but, if hurt, he didn't show it and even appeared to be amused by it. In any case it was true of most marriages, and from what I could see then, and later, my parents were not at all mismatched being less unhappily married than most couples I knew.

To be sure no term of endearment ever passed between them – certainly within my hearing – but Yiddish is poor in such expressions and even if they could have resorted to Russian (as they often did when I was about, in the mistaken belief that I couldn't follow), respectable married couples in eastern Europe simply didn't talk that way, and we would have been deeply embarrassed if they did.

One could, on the other hand, hear a great many expressions of non-endearment – in which Yiddish is particularly rich – all of them one way, directed by mother against father, but it takes two to make a quarrel and he rarely answered back, which sometimes added to her fury. *Reyd tsu em, reyd tsu der vant* – speak to him speak to the wall – was her constant refrain.

If short-tempered with father she was short-tempered with everybody, as was every Jewish housewife in Barovke, and they had a lot to be short-tempered about. I even overheard Boruch Sholem being berated by his wife, and she had a houseful of servants. In fact every Jewish housewife in Barovke was a scold, or if not they had acquired the habit of addressing their menfolk in loud, exasperated voices. That went for most non-Jewish households as well; the only exception that I knew was Soreleh Trupin.

Whenever mother was ill, father rushed to her side and tended to her lovingly. He would bring her meals on a tray and they would talk together for long hours and, as I said, when she had to go to Dvinsk for treatment, he usually went with her, and never complained of the bills she incurred, though he could ill afford them.

That in itself may be no proof of affection because father cared deeply about everyone, but he was proud of her appearance and bearing and even her snobbery – though he was also sometimes embarrassed by it – for he believed she had something to be snobbish about.

She for her part admired his learning and the standing he enjoyed in Barovke, even if she was exasperated by his incompetence, and the binding element in their personal relationship was not so much mutual affection as mutual respect.

They rarely did anything together, but that was true of most couples and certainly true of all religious couples. Even when they went out for a *spatsir* down to the lake it was usually as part of a foursome, with the two men, hands behind their back, talking gravely of grave issues, and the ladies, a few yards behind, talking lightly of light ones.

When father left Barovke and was succeeded by a young man who walked arm in arm with his wife, it occasioned a certain amount of scandal.

There was a religious reason for this. A woman is debarred from all contact with her husband for the five days of her period and the seven days which followed and, as they were always arm in arm, it suggested that either she wasn't functioning properly or that they weren't behaving properly.

In religious households men and women lived in different worlds. They had a different upbringing, a different education, and were prepared for different responsibilities.

One heard of women teachers, nurses, midwives, and there were several women shopkeepers in Barovke, mostly widows, but no one – least of all the women – questioned the belief that the true function of a woman was to be a wife, tend to her husband, look after the children and – where she was spared the years –to help out with the grandchildren.

I presume father taught my sisters the rudiments of Hebrew because they could all use a prayer book, otherwise their Jewish education was left to mother who showed them how to keep a kosher home and light the Friday night candles, and that was about all. They were, however, encouraged to acquire a sound secular education, and both worked hard and did well at school, and in many, perhaps most, Jewish households the women were a good deal more cultivated, and certainly more widely read, than the men.

Girls were introduced to domestic skills and the intricacies of needlework at an early age. Embroidery was widely admired as an

art form in eastern Europe and every house with its quota of
daughters had a ready display of embroidered tablecloths,
cushioncovers, antimacassars and wallhangings. We certainly had
a fine display in our house; and I had a large hanging by my bed
with two winged angels and the message: *steit oif in frieden* – wake
with joy.

By the time a girl was 15 or 16, she was thought of as a *kaleh-
meid* – bridal material – and if she was still single at 20, she was
spoken of as an *alte-meid* – an old maid – and would generally
move to Dvinsk to hide her shame.

There was no *shadkhan* – professional matchmaker – in
Barovke, but there were any number of amateurs and the main
social preoccupation of the place was to get the single married.
Glasgow, I was soon to discover, was no different.

Few Barovke boys married Barovke girls, possibly because they
knew each other too well, and matches were generally arranged
with people from out of town. Father frequently received letters
from colleagues or concerned parents, asking his opinion about
the son or daughter of this; or that family, and of course, about the
family itself. Father couldn't understand the whole point of the
exercise.

'Do they really expect me to tell the whole truth, or even half
the truth?' he would ask, yet always replied in glowing terms, in
florid Hebrew when addressing a colleague, in Yiddish when
addressing a layman:

' ... is a virgin of great beauty renowned for her modesty, chastity
and grace who comes from one of the most respected families in
Barovke. Her father is a good, God-fearing man who by dint of
honesty, integrity and perseverance, has built up a sizeable business
and whose home is a meeting place for the wise. Her mother is a
woman of valour who has brought up her children in the ways of
righteousness. Her grandfather, of blessed memory, was ... '

The stress placed on marriage and children meant that where a
woman failed to marry, she had no prescribed, or, indeed,
unprescribed, role in life.

In England the maiden aunt, especially in middle- and upper-
class families, is a familiar fixture and even where she is so

eccentric as to be a source of embarrassment, is never regarded as an actual misfortune. Among Jews in eastern Europe, an old maid in the family was like a death in the family, and a lingering death at that.

As far as I can remember, there were no old maids in Barovke, but there was an old bachelor, or *alter bok* as he was called.

The literal meaning of the expression is old buck, which in English suggests an ageing roué who is having too much fun to settle for domestic entanglements. In Yiddish, it suggests someone who has gone to seed without having had any fun even in his youth, and Barovke's *alter bok* was a podgy figure in a tight suit, with thick glasses, who lived with his widowed mother and would sit forlornly in the back row of the synagogue picking his nose. He could not have been much over 30.

In my younger years I naturally tagged on to mother and loved lady's night in the local bath-house – an experience I shall describe in a later chapter. And on Saturday afternoons she would visit a former teacher called Rachel who was perhaps the only Jewish woman in Barovke whom she regarded as her social equal. They were joined by four or five others and the talk was nearly always of marriage, who was going out with whom, who should be going out with whom, and who wasn't going out with anybody.

'She's nearly 17 you know.'

'Hasn't a kopek.'

'With her looks she doesn't need a kopek ... '

They all talked excitedly all at once but their voices seemed to soften as the sun began to set and the room darkened and, finally when night fell, they would rush home for *havdole* which marked the end of the holy Sabbath.

It was about mother's only formal weekly excursion, which does not mean that she was socially isolated, for people dropped in and out of each other's houses all the time.

Mother rarely read to me or told me stories, but she would sometimes sing Russian or Yiddish songs, all in minor key, all of them lachrymose in tone if not in content, so that even if they were about happy events, they left me with an unhappy feeling.

Father would pat my head, pinch my cheeks, give me small

treats and shower me with tokens of endearment which I rarely received from mother, but then in common with the rest of her family, she was undemonstrative by nature – except, that is, when she lost her temper.

According to my sisters, I could do no wrong in her eyes, she frequently prepared little treats specially for me and whenever she was away she brought back presents for me but not for them. If so, as the only son in the family – the *ben-yokhid* – I may have taken them for granted, for I haven't the vaguest recollection of them, though I do remember the many times she boxed my ears and put me early to bed.

Father, on the other hand, though always and openly affectionate, was in some ways a distant figure, partly because of the awe I had for his office and partly because I didn't see all that much of him. He left for work long before I was up in the mornings, slept in the afternoons, and would then rush off to teach the older boys in Heder, and I only had him to myself for a licensed hour when we learned together after supper.

Sometimes, when mother was unwell, he would prepare our evening meal. Mother was a good cook, he wasn't and the food was usually inedible, but he would stand over us like a mother hen to make sure we ate it. He was also endlessly solicitous if any of us showed signs of ill-health, and made sure we were adequately dressed if we showed our faces out of doors in the winter. Otherwise, if he had a free minute, he would turn to the Talmud as a drunkard turns to the bottle and I sometimes wonder, if he had not been under an obligation to teach me, whether he would have spent any length of time with me at all.

Unless there was a *bar mitzvah* or wedding to attend, we never went anywhere as a family. I would go with father to the synagogue and – when I grew older – to the bath-house. Everywhere else, a tea party, a performance by the local dramatic society, a concert in aid of some charity given by Yankele the barber and his friends, a recital by some visiting singer, I went with mother and my sisters. Shmuel Trupin, Moishe Zeitlin, even Boruch Sholem, would attend such occasions, father never. We weren't troubled by his absence because we presumed a man of his eminence had better things to do but, much as I loved father and was proud of him, I did sometimes feel that it would be nice to have a father like other fathers who were more part of this world, and less of the next one.

Chapter 5

Miserable Sinner

The centre of Barovke was built round a cobbled square which was raised slightly above the rest of the village and which was the nearest thing in the area to a hill. All the shops were in the square and in the two streets running down from it, one of which passed our house.

At the foot of the hill was the *pazharne*, the fire station, which also served as the village hall and if the synagogues were the focus of all Jewish life the *pahzharne* was the focus of all village life. It was also something of an annex to the synagogues, for parts of it were rented for the local Heder, as well as being the venue for most Jewish weddings. It was painted inside and out with dark creosote and to this day every time I smell creosote the weddings spring to mind.

As Barovke was largely built of timber, and as there were open flames everywhere – candles, kerosene lamps, hurricane lamps, spirit cookers – fires were not unknown even in winter. In the long, hot dry summers, however, homes were like tinder by the end of July, the smallest mishap could cause a major conflagration and many a night was disturbed by the cry of *pahzhar*! Fire!

As different groups in Barovke spoke different languages, when it came to an emergency only Russian sufficed and, at the cry of *pahzhar*, everyone rushed from their homes, not merely out of curiosity, but for safety, because once a fire got hold whole streets could be consumed within minutes.

According to legend, there was a fire in the 1920s which, fanned by a strong wind, destroyed half the village. Miraculously no one was killed because everybody had rushed to the lake, and stood waist-deep in water watching their homes go up in flames while ashes rained down upon them like grey snow.

I don't know if people were familiar with the idea of insuring their property, but in any case they lacked the means to do so. (We were uninsured even in Glasgow, but then for a rabbi to take out insurance would have suggested a want of confidence in the Almighty.)

We suffered a minor conflagration in our house when Anna, whose hand-rolled cigarettes burned like a flare, set fire to herself and the curtains, but mother doused her out with a bucket of water before much harm was done.

One of my sisters lost all her possessions and nearly her life in a fire which destroyed half of Kreslavka, and on summer evenings the sky would sometimes be filled with a red glow, indicating a fire in some nearby hamlet. The fires nearly always erupted after the hours of darkness, but then that was when all the candles and lamps were lit.

When we moved to Glasgow, the evening sky, summer and winter, was a bright red and I had the impression that the city was always burning until I discovered that the glow came from a steel works called Dixon Blazes.

The *pahzharniks*, firemen, were all volunteers and local heroes, and with their black leather belts, uniforms, brass buttons and brass helmets, and small hatchets in leather holsters at their side, they looked heroic (though I had never seen the hatchets used in an actual fire and I presumed they were symbols of office).

In the summer a small company of firemen would be on standby at all hours of the day and night, with horses in harness, and when the alarm sounded they would rush out with clanging bells. I often longed for a fire, preferably in someone else's house, if only to see them in action.

There was a firemen's band of which Yankel, our barber, was the star for, to our ears at least, and even to father's, he was a trumpet virtuoso. (Many years later when father heard Louis Armstrong on the radio, he said, *'Ah, er shpilt dokh vi Yankel'* – he is playing like Yankel.)

There were several Jews in Barovke who played the violin after a fashion, and one who played the double bass, but we were particularly proud of Yankel because while anyone could fiddle we generally associated wind instruments, and certainly brass, with non-Jews.

He was a lean, garrulous man with wavy hair, bright eyes and large teeth like a horse, which we presumed were the secret of his success as a trumpeter. He was not much of a barber, but then he didn't have to be, for he would crop us as a man might fleece sheep, and with as little ceremony, though he was something of a topiarist when it came to beards.

The most celebrated beard in town was that of Mendel der schwartzer, for it not so much covered his face as engulfed it and, as he was short and stocky, he was more beard than man. His eyes peered out of the undergrowth like an owl trapped in a thicket. He would drop in to Yankel's from time to time to have a path cleared to his mouth, and his ears and nostrils depilated, but he always insisted that the beard itself, his pride and his glory, remain untouched.

Mendel der geller, on the other hand, had a beard like a slab of toffee and would call in for a trim each time a hair moved out of place. Yankel's best customer, however, was his father-in-law the Cossack, who would come in once or twice a week to have his head shaved, though he was content to leave his face covered in stubble. He may also have had his head polished, for on summer days it shone like burnished copper.

Yankel was overwhelmed on market days and was busy on the approaches to the Jewish festivals, but one always knew of his slack times when one heard the melancholy sound of his trumpet echoing across the square.

He was at his happiest in uniform in the firemen's band which sometimes gave concerts in the *pahzharne* on winter evenings, and augmented the army band in the village square on Tzitsego Mayo.

The *pahzharne* was also the venue of the local amateur dramatic society which was entirely composed of young women, for father would not have allowed them to perform together with young men. In any case it was generally felt that young men had – or should have – better things to do.

A little downhill from the *pahzharne* stood the *atkhozha*, a recent addition to public amenities, which, when the wind swung our way, was a public nuisance, especially in summer. It was a public lavatory, a large multi-seated version of the wooden privies to be found in every back garden and was built to serve the local market.

Thursday was market day and if Barovke was a *shtetaleh* on other days of the week, it became something of a *shtot* on Thursdays, as farmers and tradesmen, buyers and sellers from Tartak, Yode, Schwinchyan, Kanist and other surrounding hamlets, crowded in with their horses and wagons, filling the square and overflowing into the surrounding streets.

Whatever language one spoke the dominant sound in the market was Russian. There was much haggling in loud voices and deals were finally clinched with spitting on palms and hearty handshakes.

The market was at its most exciting in the winter when people came in sledges rather than wagons. Clouds of steam rose from every mouth and formed a mist over the market, while the horses' urine cut golden channels in the thick snow.

The peasants were large, robust, hearty figures and with their sheepskin coats, knee-length boots, bushy beards and tall fur hats they looked like giants.

Though most men were bearded, Jewish beards with the exception of the two Mendels tended to be thin and straggly and grew downwards, while Gentile beards grew outwards with a wild exuberance.

There were no taverns in Jewish Barovke, nor anywhere else as far as I remember, but vodka was readily available in the surrounding shops, and there was a good deal of drunkenness, which didn't really matter as long as the horses were sober.

The biggest drunk in the district was the local vet, a large, unkempt German in a loud tweed suit, who came in a neat little two-wheeler pulled by a neat little horse. He was a terrifying figure with a red steaming face, bulging bloodshot eyes and a hoarse voice, and would rent the air with curses.

He was much in demand on market days and every time he treated an animal he would exchange drinks with his client so that, by the time he finished he was on the point of collapse, and sometimes did collapse and was taken to recover in the *pahzharne*.

Father was also kept busy because many of the traders and some of the farmers were Jewish and they would bring in chickens or sheep to be slaughtered, or come in to ask a *shaila* – some point of religious law – or to settle a dispute. He was also frequently asked to *opshprekhen an eyn hore*, to exorcize the evil eye.

Jewish life in eastern Europe was steeped in superstition. Even those who did not believe in God seemed to believe in the devil and the power of the evil eye and whenever they praised a child for his good looks or an adult for his good fortune they would add – as some still do – almost unthinkingly, *keyn eyn hore*, may the evil eye not perceive it. And thus when someone suffered a grave illness or some other misfortune, the victim or a relative would call on the local rabbi for his intervention.

Father did not have a tariff for such services, but he always received a little something, and where he effected a cure he received quite a lot. In that respect he was not as well placed as Dr Heller, who charged the same whether he was successful or not, but to an extent we lived on the evil eye.

I never discovered what formulae father uttered to frustrate the evil eye. He did not like to talk about it, and was plainly embarrassed by it. I presume he did not believe it himself, but he could not dismiss it out of hand, not because it was a minor source of income, but because many eminent rabbis and most of his contemporaries took it seriously. Father was perfectly prepared to take on the modern world and point out the error of its ways, but he was not the sort of man to challenge a consensus among his colleagues.

In any case the belief in the evil eye was built into many a venerable tradition, so that when a couple became engaged their parents would shatter a plate to avert the evil eye and, to this day, bridegrooms shatter a glass underfoot during the wedding ceremony for the same reason.

I was deeply superstitious myself. We had a privy situated well away from the house at the end of a rutted field, which was a source of fear and apprehension to me. It didn't trouble me during daylight hours, but Zamke Zussman who, drawing on what he said were ancient Jewish texts, warned me that once night descended, the privy teemed with demons who could climb up your anus. Leipkaleh assured me it was all nonsense, but I was nevertheless terrified of using the privy after dark and during the long winter nights I suffered from voluntary constipation.

I loved the Jewish world, but sometimes felt imprisoned by it, and found markets and market days particularly exhilarating because they were the one time of the week when I had a passing sensation of belonging to a larger, more open and more boisterous universe.

Friday mornings were also busy, and sometimes frantic, in preparation for the Sabbath. Few homes had sizeable pantries or larders, or the money to stock them. Food was bought as and when it was needed but as Sabbath approached the need was considerable for one often had guests. One was required to celebrate the day with three festive meals and there were families who half starved themselves during the week to celebrate God's beneficence on the Sabbath.

It was also said that one had a *neshomo yeseiro* – supplementary soul – on the Sabbath, but whether one did or not, one ate as if one had a supplementary body, and there was always a last-minute rush to the shops for candles, butter, sugar, boot polish, boot laces, fly paper, salt.

Things gradually quietened down in the afternoon as the shops emptied and every male in Barovke made for the bath-house.

Judaism has never claimed that cleanliness was next to godliness but it does insist on minimal levels of hygiene which become operative from the moment one wakes:

'When a man arises from his sleep he must not walk four cubits unless he has washed his hands ... at least as far as the joint of his fingers ... and while drying his hands must intone the blessing: "Blessed art thou, O Lord our God, King of the universe, who hast sanctified us by thy commandments, and commanded us concerning the washing of hands."'

One is also required to wash one's hands and make a blessing before each and every meal and after using the toilet. Opinion was divided whether one was also required to wash after a fart. Father ruled that one was. I am not sure whether his ruling applied to both farter and fartees, but there was a great deal of hand washing after the heavy Sabbath meals.

As the laws of hygiene were originally formulated when most Jews lived in the orient, water was used sparingly and the drawback to washing by law is that small boys, certainly, tended to be satisfied with the minimal requirements so that while we had clean hands – at least as far as the joints of our fingers – we were not otherwise over-washed. This hardly mattered in the long hot days of summer when we enjoyed a semi-aquatic existence and spent much of our time splashing around in the mill stream, mill pond and lake. In the winter, however, a room full of small boys could turn the air black, and were it not for our weekly visits to the bath-house we would have had grass growing in our ears.

I don't know what, if anything, went on in the bath-house on the other days and nights of the week, but Thursday night was lady's night, while Fridays were sacred to men.

When we first came to Barovke I usually went with my mother and sisters on Thursday night which I much preferred to the men-only sessions on Friday, for I preferred the look of the women. They were softer, smoother, rounder and whiter.

Being short I tended to identify them by their pubic hair. Hannah Ratz, for example, had hair like shredded carrots, her mother-in-law Bashke's was a yellowish-white, like the beard of a heavy smoker, while Soreleh Trupin's was jet black, well kempt and neatly shaped, like an eye-patch.

As I grew taller – and I must have grown quickly – I became aware of bosoms, their huge size and the way they changed shape with every change in posture, and the whole event was a boisterous social occasion. Women stood around chatting, children ran around playing, and washing was almost a secondary matter. The dominant smell was of rotting timber and carbolic, but tempered by the passing fragrance of perfumed soap and toilet water.

It all ended abruptly when a small girl opened her legs and invited me to enter, and I did just that there and then. I may have been backward in some respects, but was precocious in others. I don't know who walloped me round the ears, my mother or hers, though nobody lifted a finger against my temptress, and I was taken home half-dried.

Not a word was said either then or later, but thereafter I went to the bath-house with father, which was a totally different experience and infinitely less pleasant.

For a start, it was grimly functional. Father had a long *matzalke*, a loofah, with the texture of wire-wool which might have been specifically designed to flay a person alive.

Father was normally the gentlest of men, but he would rub the loofah down with a harsh soap which mother normally used for scrubbing the floor and apply it to me with an angry fury, as if discharging all the pent-up frustrations he had suffered during the week, and left me raw, red, sore, crying for mercy and gasping for breath, and I was not so much cleaned as purged.

Worse than that, however, was the dreaded steam room, but there my pains were self-inflicted.

The room consisted of a series of broad wooden steps, and the higher one climbed, the hotter and denser the steam. Father, with a broom of birch twigs in hand began on the third step, paused a little, went on to the fourth, the fifth, the sixth, till he finally vanished, like Moses on Sinai, in a cloud of steam on the seventh, and all one could hear was the whack of birch twigs on bare flesh, and muffled cries of pain – or was it ecstasy?

I was never required to follow him, but all the gang was there and under the guidance of Zamke Zussman, we engaged in a weekly endurance test to see who could climb higher and stay longer.

Shaike Trupin was excused because he was too delicate. The

rest of us had to follow, and follow we did. Zamke made it as far as the fifth step, and stayed for several minutes. Welfke and Shmulik got as far as the fourth. I made it as far as the third, and stayed for some seconds, and we all emerged looking like newly poached lobsters.

Once out of the steam room father dunked himself briefly in the pool and went home as soon as he dried himself, but most men would go outside to sit around in the grass in what was known as *die nakiteh duma* – the naked forum – for a chat and a smoke.

Beirach Fleischman, who would generally preside over the occasion with a large *yarmulke* on his head and a cigarette in his mouth, looked like a thoroughly unfrocked priest.

Beirach travelled a lot, was widely read and was generally regarded. He certainly regarded himself as an authority on the outside world, and the naked forum was not concerned with gossip, small talk or anything parochial. People spoke in earnest tones of earnest issues, as if, once reduced to their bare essentials, they had no time for frivolities.

On hot afternoons the air was filled with mosquitoes, black flies and horse-flies and the exchanges were accompanied by much slapping and scratching – especially of crotches – which did not, however, impair the gravity of the occasion and it was there that I heard of such names as Stalin, Roosevelt, Baldwin, Mussolini, Pilsudski, Jabotinsky and Weizman.

The bath-house was not so far from the centre of Barovke that the naked forum couldn't be seen by people with sharp eyes, especially when – as was the case with Hannah Ratz – they also had binoculars.

Father never took part in the forum but had to field any number of complaints about it, and after the service on Saturday mornings he would appeal to the congregants that if they had to appear naked in public they should at least turn their backs to the village. He would also intercede personally with Beirach.

Beirach, though one of father's most loyal disciples, was unco-operative on this issue, and unrepentant, and would make his point in a sing-song voice as if arguing over a page of the Talmud:

'Forgive me Reb Azriel, but first of all, they don't have to look. If they do look, they won't see anything they haven't seen before, but if they haven't seen it before, then it's about time they did see it.'

Apart from the trouble at the bath-house there was trouble at the lake, and for the same reason, though the lake was outside the village and out of sight.

Nobody in Barovke used bathing suits and most of us hadn't even heard of them. There was a general tradition that women and children used the lake during the day while the men used it in the evening or first thing in the morning – father went for his swim at the crack of dawn – but nobody seemed to be sure when the day finished and the evening began and who, or what, constituted a child. That too fell into father's domain and, long before the summer was over he found himself praying for the onset of winter. (Though there could be trouble even in winter. Binyomin Rosin, the Cossack, liked to roll himself in the snow after a steam bath, and given his build he could be seen from miles away.)

Father had his problems even on the Sabbath, but they stemmed from a different quarter.

Mother, though not always industrious at other times of the week, was a whirling fury on Friday, cooking, baking, cleaning, scrubbing, and when it came to the evening she liked to collapse but was rarely free to do so because Jewish tradition demanded that one should have a guest at the Sabbath table, where possible. In Barovke it was always possible and nearly every Friday evening father would return with some bedraggled figure in tow, a *meshulakh* usually, who was collecting money for a *yeshiva*, an orphanage, a home for the blind, or some other worthy cause.

There was no shortage of worthy causes in the Jewish world, even if there was a shortage of money, and there was a constant traffic of *meshulokhim*, as the collectors were known, through every *shtot*, *shtetl* and *shtetaleh* in eastern Europe, though by the time they reached a place like Barovke, they were scraping fairly near the bottom of the barrel.

They were all bearded, all in black and all came armed with letters of recommendation from leading rabbis, and elaborate receipt books, both of which were sometimes fraudulent, but father felt that if a man was so desperate as to forge such documents he was truly in need, and he didn't look too closely at their credentials.

They were not always prepossessing and usually travel-stained and when we sat down to our meal they would dive on the food as if they hadn't eaten for a week, which they probably hadn't. 'Where do you find them?' mother would ask, 'under a rock?'

I was usually in bed long before they left, but I could hear the exchanges from my parents' bedroom.

'*Ken ikh not hobn a minutes rue?* – can't I have a minute's rest?'

'*S'i doch a mitsve* – but it's a commandment.'

'*Du hargest mir avek mit deyne mitsves* – you're killing me with your commandments.'

But it was not only a matter of commandments. Father did not get much stimulation from our company, for we were young, and he did not have all that much to say to mother, not because she was stupid or we were querulous but because she was a woman, and he often quoted the Talmudic precept that one should limit one's conversation with females. Not that he had all that much to say to males but, when he had a Talmud *khokhem*, a scholar, at table – and some of the *meshullochim* were genuine scholars – he was a different man. His eyes brightened, he became animated, for it not only enabled him to display his own knowledge, it was an opportunity to learn something new. He also loved an argument over some obscure point of Jewish law which brought back happy memories of Slobodka where he had spent whole days in disputations. If such occasions were stimulating for father, however, they were a dreadful bore for the rest of us and especially for mother.

One *meshullach*, a fairly learned man with a long grey beard, who had been our guest on several occasions, said he was too old to continue with his job and asked father if he would like to take over from him.

'You go to interesting places, meet interesting people and can make a good living,' he said, 'depending, of course, on how much you raise.'

Now father, as I have said, hated cutting throats and the sight of blood, even chicken's blood. He also loved travel and I suspect may have welcomed the idea of getting away from mother – and perhaps even us – from time to time, but when he put the idea to mother she was brutally frank.

'Look,' she said, 'you never even knew how to get money out of people who owed you money, what hope have you got of raising money from people who don't?' Which settled the matter.

On Friday night father came home with a man with a red nose and magnificent beard who was reeking of vodka, and who, in the course of the meal, made a pass at mother, so for a month or two we were blessedly free of visitors, but habit was the better part of father' religion – as it is of mine. He also had a stern sense of duty, and the *meshullochim* soon returned.

The Sabbath day was more restful.

The two synagogues in Barovke were known respectively as the small one and the large one, and father went to the first on Friday night and the second on Saturday mornings and afternoons. Mother would rarely attend either but then few women did. He only gave a sermon about five times a year so that his duties were not onerous and when we got back home he would make the necessary blessings, and sit down to a glass – a fairly large one – of vodka, and a small plate of baked herring.

He knocked back his vodka in a gulp, as if it was a particularly nasty medicine, which is precisely what it tasted like to me. Boruch Sholem would sometimes bring round a bottle of French cognac, which at least had a pleasant fragrance, which he knocked back in the same way. It was only when he was presented with a bottle of what he called 'English cognac' and which, I presume, must have been Scotch whisky, that he began to take his liquor sip by sip.

Main meals were always at lunch time and on the Sabbath and festivals they were always heavy and prolonged, and never consisted of less than four courses and sometimes stretched to five or six.

One began with chopped herring, chopped liver, or *gefilte* fish or *putcha*, and sometimes all four. Chicken soup with *lokshen* or dumplings came next, followed by *cholent* and *kugel* and finally and inevitably, there was compote, which always consisted of a pair of prunes in a plate of apple sauce, like sad eyes in a plate face.

The most celebrated Jewish dishes, *gefilte* fish and *cholent* arose out of the need to make expensive ingredients – namely fish and meat – go a long way. The former consisted of one part fish – usually carp or pike – to three or four parts of bread, apples and onion, while the latter consisted of a few strips of brisket and several spoonfuls of *schmaltz* in a huge quantity of potaoes and beans, baked together in a large cast-iron pot, in a slow oven.

There was no such thing in Barovke as a fast oven, but slow ovens could be made slower by being banked with ashes, and the *cholent* was in the oven for some 20 hours before it was ready for consumption and, in many instances, was heated and reheated for further consumption during the rest of the week.

In winter, when the days were short and there was a third meal – the *salehs seudah* – to be crammed in, lunches were hurried, but in the summer they seemed to take hours, and we – which is to say Father and I – would sing hymns between each course while my mother and sisters cleared away one set of dishes and brought in another.

When the compote was served, father would test me on what I had learned in the course of the week, which struck me as a gratuitous exercise, because he was my principal teacher. It was not a rigorous test but I got impatient with the questions because I could by then hear the sounds of my friends at play in the streets outside, and we still had the long *birkas hamozon*, the grace after meals, to complete.

In some respects my favourite Sabbath meal was the *salehs seudah*. In culinary terms, it was perfunctory, a few slices of bread, some *gefilte* fish with horseradish, and perhaps the leftovers from mother's compote. In our house, for some reason, they were men-only occasions and father would have two or three of his cronies round, Shimshon Ber, Boruch Sholem, Beirach, and there would be more singing – of Psalms usually – than eating, and father would say what he called a *vertle* – a mini-word – on the *sedrah*, the weekly portion from Scripture.

On Friday night the dining room was bright with the glow of candles and kerosene lamps. On Sabbath day itself, one depended on natural light, what there was of it, and there wasn't much because windows were small and, in our case, obscured by cherry trees.

The *salehs seudah* was always eaten at dusk and, in the summer, as the day darkened and the evening mists swirled in through the open windows, I could almost see the Shechinah – the Divine Presence – hovering over our small assembly.

The Shechinah never seemed to be about when there were women present, possibly because they were too much part of this world, and dissipated the mood of sanctity necessary to invoke It!

Once the meal was over we made our unhurried way to synagogue for the evening prayers and returned for the *havdoloh* ceremony which separated the Holy Sabbath from the profane week.

The ceremony was fairly elaborate and the entire household would assemble for it.

There was one blessing over wine – though as we couldn't afford wine, we used milk – another over spices, and a third over candles, followed by the prayer:

'Blessed art thou O Lord King of the Universe who separates the holy from the profane, light from darkness, Israel from the other nations, between the seventh day and the six working days ... '

Mother would follow with a prayer in Yiddish specially designed for women:

'May Elijah the prophet enter our homes, heal the sick, bless the healthy, and save us from dependence on anyone ... '

And finally there would be songs including a bleak little Yiddish ditty, sung as always in a minor key:

> *Geyt avek der Shabbes koydesh, es is dokh sheyn nit gut*
> *es is dokh umetik oyfn hartzen.*
> *Vayter mit di lates, vayter mit di shmates, vayter mit dem ayzun der*
> *schvartzen.*

(Once the holy Sabbath is over, one no longer feels good.
The heart becomes melancholy.
Back to the rags, back to the patches, back to the black iron.)

It probably began as a tailor's song, but both the tune and the words conveyed the sense of desolation which so often follows euphoria. One felt like Cinderella after the ball.

As one is not allowed to wash dishes on the Sabbath itself, the womenfolk busied themselves cleaning all the great piles of dirty pots and pans, cutlery and crockery which had accumulated during the day. Father would comfort himself with a cigarette and the Talmud. I was sent to bed.

In spite of my immersion in sanctity and my docile demeanour, I was by the age of eight showing incipient signs of becoming a *yungatsh* – a young ruffian. I didn't always wash my hands before meals, and didn't always say the grace after meals, or said it in attenuated form, and instead of spending half an hour over my morning prayers I would rush through them at the double in ten minutes.

I also began raising awkward questions during my daily study periods with father. Thus, for example, when we came to the story of Noah's ark I asked:

'Wouldn't the lions have eaten Noah and his family?'

'They were in different compartments.'

'Wouldn't they have eaten the cows?'

'They were also in different compartments.'

'Wouldn't the cats have eaten the mice?'

'They were also in different compartments.'

'There must have been a lot of compartments.'

'There were.'

'It must have been a big ark.'

'It was.'

'But it says here it was 300 cubits long, 50 cubits broad and 30 cubits high. How big is a cubit?'

'Big enough.'

Father didn't normally resent questions. If anything he encouraged them, for they showed I was awake and alert – which

I sometimes wasn't – but in this instance he suspected that I had obtained my questions secondhand from Leipkaleh – his prize pupil – which I had.

Leipkaleh had also told me that by his calculations the ark was no bigger than our house, and that even if all the animals could somehow have been crammed on board, it would have sunk under their weight, but that was not a matter which I cared to bring up with father. Asking heretical questions was one thing, making a heretical statement was quite another.

And then came the Black Sabbath.

There were, as I have said, three statutory meals to the Sabbath, but there was a further tradition which, though not statutory, was of ancient pedigree, the *shabbes-shlof*, when people sagging under the weight of their midday meal, would retire to bed for their siesta. And thus while our elders slept the sweet sleep of the pious, and the curtains billowed with their snores, we had Barovke to ourselves.

There were many things which were forbidden on the Sabbath and one of them is swimming, but if someone falls into the water one can – indeed one must – go in after him. And thus when the hot days came, we would make for the mill pond, strip, one of us would fall – or be pushed – into the water, and the rest of us would dive in after him. We didn't bring towels, which would have suggested premeditation, but dried out in the sun.

There was, however, one period of the year when we could not allow ourselves such liberties, and this was the three weeks – extending from about the middle of July till the first week in August – which commemorated the siege of Jerusalem and the destruction of the Temple about 2,500 years before we were born.

The three weeks are climaxed by the nine days, which culminate in the Fast of Ab, in which swimming was forbidden even on weekdays, but then came the hottest Sabbath anyone could remember, and it was the Sabbath before the fast, one of the most solemn days of the year.

The air quivered with heat, and even the trees seemed to sag, and before us lay the mill pond, cool, clear and inviting, with dragonflies buzzing among the reeds. We looked around to see if

the coast was clear, as it always was, and without a further thought
threw off our clothes, and dived into the water.

When I came up for air a minute later who should I see but
three bearded figures in black approaching.

The others grabbed their clothes and ran but I, the rabbi's son,
was afraid I might be identified. I dived under again, and stayed
under for as long as I could, but when, with lungs bursting I
finally surfaced, they were there right by the bank, and could not
have been more surprised if I had been Aphrodite.

That was not my first serious transgression, and would not be
my last.

A few months earlier, during the festival of Passover – which
lasts eight days – a bus line was opened to Dvinsk. It was a great,
even historic occasion in the life of Barovke, and Passover or not,
half the Jews in the neighbourhood and all the children assembled
in the village square to witness the great event. Others were
scattered along the paved highway which led to Dvinsk and Tolk
and, on horseback, trotted back and forward to make sure the
highway itself was clear.

There was a military band on one dais, and several important
personages, some of them in one uniform or another, and then as
the bus – a magnificent object, large and powerful with a steaming
radiator and an exhaust like gunfire – came in sight, we all gave a
loud cheer while the band struck up the grand march from *Aida*.

A minute later a burly, red-faced, white-haired figure
descended who I at first thought was Karlis Ulmanis. He shook
hands with the figures on the dais, and then made a prepared
speech.

It was a great day for Latvia and Barovke, he said, and the
journey to Dvinsk, which by horse and cart took the better part of
a day, would now be completed in just over an hour. The isolation
of Barovke was over. It was now linked with the heart of Latvia.

There were more cheers and, while the band played another
march, an assistant handed him a large bag, from which he
distributed bars of English chocolate among all the children in the
square, and we scattered in all directions with loud whoops of joy,
bearing our trophies aloft.

I don't remember the make of the chocolate, but I do remember the two dominoes on the wrapper. I couldn't wait to show it to my sisters, but then when I was nearly home, father emerged in his festive wear and I suddenly remembered it was Passover and there I was with chocolate in my hand.

Now if the Jewish dietary laws are fairly strict in the course of the year, they are impossibly strict on Passover. At other times everything is kosher unless it is expressly forbidden. On Passover everything is forbidden unless it is expressly permitted, and chocolate – except where it is made under strict rabbinical supervision – is forbidden, and I was afraid that father might tell me to destroy it forthwith.

Instead he proved to be lenient, and told me to put it in the attic and eat it once Passover had passed over

Unfortunately, it was only the second day of the festival. There were six more to go. I got through the first day without much difficulty but after that the thought of the chocolate mouldering in the attic tormented my waking hours and disturbed what should have been my sleeping hours, so one afternoon while alone in the house I sneaked up to the attic and wolfed the bar.

When the festival was over my younger sister asked if I wasn't going to get the chocolate.

'The chocolate?'

'The English chocolate you got from the bus, aren't you going to give me some?'

'Ah, the chocolate.'

I lit a candle, went up to the attic and returned some twenty minutes later looking dusty and dishevelled.

'Can't find it. The mice must have eaten it.'

My parents exchanged glances, but didn't say a word. I had shown myself to be not only a glutton, but a liar and pretty poor liar at that.

They had a problem on their hands.

Chapter 6

Toilers and Tailors

The local economy was all but self-sufficient. Dairy foods, milk, butter, eggs, cream, were abundant and cheap in the summer, and inexpensive in the winter while eggs in particular were so plentiful that we used them as grenades in our army games.

The trouble with dairy foods in the summer, of course, was that they wouldn't keep. Refrigerators were unheard of and few homes even had cold larders. Many people had goats and not a few had cows and they were more or less used as larders, which is to say the poor beasts were milked not when they needed milking, but when their owners needed milk. Even then it would often go off and in the summer one had sour milk with everything, sour milk with borscht, sour milk with potatoes, herrings in sour milk, sour milk with sugar and cinnamon, and sour milk with *shtshavel*, a weed as common in eastern Europe as nettles, and some even made an excellent soup out of nettles (with sour milk, of course). A weed had to be lethal before it was dismissed as inedible.

In the summer too there were pillowslips full of sour milk, like great bloated udders, dripping from every tree as it turned slowly into cream cheese, while the ground beneath them turned white and then green and then solid and whole flocks of crows would peck at it in the early morning. And it is cream cheese which in turn provides the twin glories of Jewish culinary art, cheese blintzes and cheesecake.

Every Jewish festival has its own traditional fare and the traditional fare on Shavuot (Pentecost) which is celebrated seven weeks after Passover, is cheesecake and blintzes. Rabbis have ascribed deep mystical reasons to the tradition and derive innumerable homilies from it, but Shavuot happens to be a summer festival, and in the summer cream cheese is cheap and abundant. In fact it was the only form of cheese available. I didn't taste hard cheese until I came to Glasgow.

Nearly every house in Barovke stood in its own small plot of land and was shaded by apple and cherry trees. Many people grew their own vegetables and some – as we did – rented small strips of land in which they grew potatoes and cabbage, so that fruit and vegetables were cheap and abundant in season, and once anything was out of season it was not only out of reach but out of consideration. Few people took the trouble to grow flowers, except possibly sunflowers, and the blooms we had on our table on the Sabbath and festivals were all wildflowers garnered by me from the nearby fields. It was one of my many Friday afternoon tasks. Another was to cut up old newspapers into neat squares for use in the privy, which was situated well away from the house at the end of a rutted field.

Every household had a large brass pan on the wall which served as an ornament during the year and was used in the summer to make *kluvnick* – strawberry jam – and though some people actually grew strawberries they were mostly picked in the wild, and one had strawberry jam all the year round.

Some people made a rich, syrupy wine out of raisins or cherries fermenting in large jars of sugar, though the nearest thing to a national drink was *kvas*, while *kvas mit zoshe* – kvas and soda – was the nectar of the gods.

Cabbages – *kapusta* – were diced, sprinkled with caraway seeds, and preserved in a barrel as a winter food and served up hot or cold. Gherkins were pickled in dill and eaten as an accompaniment to meat or fish or as a delicacy in its own right.

Corn was grown locally, ground locally and used locally and

mother seemed to spend half her life, her face covered in flour,
pounding dough, kneading and rolling it. When she rolled it for
bread and cakes it was a minor matter, but when she rolled it for
lokshen, *farfel* or other forms of pasta, she reduced it to a fine film
which covered the entire kitchen table. She would leave it to dry
for a while, and then fold it and re-fold it like a tablecloth and cut
it into strips. There was a baker in Barovke, but I don't know how
he made a living because every house had a brick-lined oven like
a brick kiln which was banked in the summer, stocked in the
winter but kept going all the year round, and every housewife
baked her own bread, *challas* and cakes. The bread was black with
an indentation at the centre, like a navel. The *challah* – made for
the Sabbath and festivals – was white and glossed with eggs. The
cakes came in three forms, *bulkas*, which were Danish pastries;
lekakh (honey cake) and *torte* (sponge cake), and again they were
made only for the Sabbath and festivals. When mother was unwell
we would sometimes buy white bread for her from Mitrofannoff's
in Dvinsk who made weekly deliveries in a horse-drawn van.
When I came to Glasgow and saw people eating white bread on
weekdays I presumed they were invalids.

All three kosher butchers seemed fairly busy and every Jewish
house had a roll of *wursht* dangling in the kitchen, like every
Christian house had a crucifix and when I was small I thought it
had some religious significance. Perhaps it does. It would
certainly make a striking fertility symbol, and could also be used
as a weapon.

Fish were caught locally and sold live and I have a vivid
memory of little Bashke Ratz struggling home from market with
a huge frisky pike clasped to her bosom and wrestling it to the
ground before finally bringing it under control.

Even if local, fish were thought of as a luxury and served only
on the Sabbath and festivals.

Every part of the fish was eaten, including the head, and the
bones were sucked dry before being passed on to the cat. There
were many cats in Barovke, but few fat cats.

Anything from out of town, and certainly from out of the
country, was prohibitively expensive and the only imported goods

in common use were mustard, tea, chicory, cocoa and lemons.

I was later told that herrings were likewise imported, which was rather surprising, for herrings, potatoes and bread, along with chicken fat and goose fat – or *schmaltz* – formed the staple diet.

Herrings, certainly, were the main source of protein, and came in many forms, baked, pickled, soused, smoked, served up with sour cream, or chopped with onions, apples and stale bread. On the Sabbath they were treated as an hors d'oeuvre. On weekdays they formed the main course and often the only course, though it was only when we came to Scotland that we discovered that herrings – in the form of kippers – could also be enjoyed at breakfast. Breakfast in Barovke consisted of chicory and a roll, sometimes with butter, sometimes with jam, but never with butter and jam.

We sometimes turned to smoked buckling from Dvinsk by way of a change, but the only tinned food which seemed readily available was smoked sprats from Riga. (I virtually lived on them and red caviare during my first visit to the Soviet Union in 1972, and washed them down with *kvasch*.)

When there was an important visitor in Barovke, father would have a *kiddush* at home after the Sabbath morning service and mother would put out a couple of bottles of schnapps, cakes, pickled gherkins and perhaps half a dozen varieties of herring. The herring went quicker than the schnapps.

Kiddush means sanctification, which is to say father made a blessing before corks were drawn, and thus elevated a booze-up to the status of a holy communion.

It is totally untrue that Jews don't drink, but they rarely get drunk because they eat when they're drinking, and because they usually bring God into the act which in itself induces a certain sobriety.

Mother made our own bedding, pillows, quilts – or *perines*, as we called them – and mattresses out of feathers and down which father brought from the slaughter house. It was, I suppose, one of the perks of his calling. Washing and drying them was quite a job, but when one sank into bed one vanished from view and had a mild sensation of drowning. I don't know if they were good for the

back, but they were marvellously comfortable, and portable (if
bulky). When we left for Glasgow mother sold almost everything
we had, but took the *perines* with her. They lasted until well after
the war and it took me a long time to get used to normal bedding.

Nearly all homes had sewing machines and many had spinning
wheels and the dominant sound when walking through Barovke
on a summer evening when windows were thrown open, was the
crying of children and the clatter of treadles. On the long, balmy
summer nights women would sit out on the verandahs in small
groups, knitting, stitching, darning, chatting.

Rooms were small and ceilings were low and after the intense
heat of the day bedrooms were like ovens and I dreaded bedtime
on summer nights. As always I invoked the names of Michael,
Gabriel, Uriel and Raphael to lull me to sleep but it didn't always
work in the summer and near voices and far, with the occasional
burst of laughter, and even distant strains of music played on a
mandolin or accordion, came wafting in through the open
window. Someone, somewhere, was having fun and I, as usual,
was out of it.

When we were young mother made nearly all our clothes – and
possibly her own – and knitted our socks, scarves, gloves,
cardigans and jumpers, to say nothing of cushion covers,
antimacassars and bedspreads. It was uncommon to encounter a
woman without her balls of wool, knitting needles or crochet
hook. The first time I went on a bus to Dvinsk there were about a
dozen women in the seats on either side, all of them working away
with knitting needles and crochet hooks like instrumentalists in a
band. On the Sabbath and festivals when such work was forbidden, mother didn't know what to do with her hands.

My first memory of distress arose out of mother's tailoring. She
made my trousers with elasticated tops without buttons or flies,
which didn't worry me at all till I noticed that while the other boys
unbuttoned their flies like men when they wanted a pee, I had to
pull my trousers down. One of them even remarked that I was
wearing *meydlishe koyzu*, girls' knickers.

I ran home in tears and demanded trousers with buttons and a
fly. I was surprised at my own assertiveness for it was unlike me

to demand anything. Mother must have been equally surprised for she made them there and then, though the buttons were small and fiddly and I had no end of difficulty doing them up or – what was more important – undoing them.

During the week we had a *tserat* – a heavy oilcloth as a table cover, which must have been imported. On the Sabbath and festivals we used damask tablecloths handmade by a local weaver.

The rich – in so far as there were any in Barovke – could buy ready-made English shoes in Tzeitlins. The rest of us had to make do with handmade shoes, or more usually boots, from Yossel, Leipkaleh's father. If one wanted to brighten his day one only had to ask how Leipkaleh was doing, though he would sometimes volunteer the information even if one didn't ask.

Among Orthodox Jews when there is a death in the family the male next of kin do not shave for a month – *shloshim* – by way of mourning. Yossel always looked in mourning because he rarely shaved. On the other hand he did not seem disposed to grow a beard either and with his thick bristle and small bright eyes he looked like an overgrown hedgehog.

He was a short man with broad shoulders and only made shoes' uppers. Someone else made the soles. Both produced work of the highest quality and were possibly victims of their own craftsmanship because a pair of their boots lasted – or at least were made to last – for life so that both lived in poverty.

The four tailors did rather better, for while one could wear the same boots Sabbath and weekdays, one needed a special suit for the Sabbath and a good, heavy overcoat for the long winter months. All four had the habit of looking you up and down, as if they were measuring you up for a suit. Although Ratz was the best and most expensive, one could haggle with him, as one haggled with everyone.

Essential foodstuffs had their known prices, but otherwise quoted prices were presumed to be notional and were often fanciful so that anyone who didn't haggle laid himself open to robbery. Father felt that haggling was beneath him, but mother, as the daughter of a trader, revelled in it and he left all business transactions to her.

There were two *kapelush-makhers* – cap-makers – in Barovke.
Both did rather well because no one went hatless in the winter
and Jews had their heads covered all the year round. A few people
owned grey or beige fedoras which were made in Dvinsk or Riga.
Most people wore black caps with shiny visors which were made
locally. Fur hats were mandatory in the winter, usually with flaps
which could be extended over the ears.

There was also one milliner, a tall, thin, starchy dame with
silvery hair piled high on her head, whose house was full of
German, English and French fashion magazines. They must have
been well out of date for the hats she made, with their broad brims
and large feathers, evoked memories of Old Vienna. She looked
out of place in Barovke, and so did her creations, and there was
in any case little call for hats. Young women if they had their heads
covered at all, wore berets. Older ones went bare headed in the
summer or wore a shawl in the winter. There was, however, one
day which called for hats, and that was Yom Kippur. Were it not
for Yom Kippur the milliner would have starved.

Mother, as the rabbi's wife, should, in keeping with the Jewish
laws of modesty, have had her hair covered night and day. She
wore a small black hat with a piece of netting over her eyes –
which gave her a Mata Hari look – on the rare occasions she went
to synagogue, and would don a kerchief when we had a visiting
rabbi in the house, but otherwise remained bare headed.

Apart from the shopkeepers and artisans there were any
number of people in Barovke who described themselves rather
grandly as *haendlers* – merchants – though they had no shops,
offices, warehouses or any visible means of support and were away
for most of the week. Some – like Chatzkel with-the-six-sons – did
well. Others, like Beirach, did badly. Some did very badly, and
depended on charity handouts to see them through the Sabbath
and festivals.

There were three or four Jewish farmers in the neighbourhood
who tended a few acres, and we were not quite sure what to call
them, and they were not always sure how to describe themselves.
There were no large farmers about, and the Yiddish for a small
farmer or peasant was *poyer*, which was also another word for *goy*,

but while a *goy* was simply a non-Jew, a *poyer* was a boor, coarse, illiterate, brutal and stupid, which may suggest what Jews – and others – thought of peasants. But it was not a way in which Jewish farmers, no matter how small, cared to be described.

The only Jewish farmer I came across was a dour, lean leathery figure, with puttees like grubby bandages which went up to his knees. One rarely saw him in synagogue, but he had a considerable number of cows, goats and sheep and when their milk dried up or they failed to reproduce, instead of calling in the vet he would ask father for his blessing. I suppose father was cheaper, though he may also have been more effective.

If I remember rightly, he also kept pigs, though if he did he never invoked father's help for their welfare. He was semi-literate and my sisters helped him with the many forms which were then already beginning to blight the life of the farmer.

I regarded him with a certain amount of awe. For a start he owned a horse, not like Zussman's broken-down hack, but a well-groomed, handsome healthy beast which could have served in a cavalry unit. His landholding, though small, was not contiguous and he would travel from strip to strip on horseback, and looked rather impressive when he did. He knew how to tend to cattle and goats, could plough, sow and reap, measure up land, assess the quality of a crop, mend machinery and was also a fairly proficient builder. About the only thing he couldn't do was smile and he went about his day with a look of suppressed fury on his face.

Many Jews farmed in a small way, a very small way, which is to say they had small strips of land and kept a goat or two tethered in the surrounding fields or browsing among the vegetation which flanked the footpaths.

Goats had a unique place in Jewish lore. They feature in many folk-songs, and the most famous of them – a kid for two farthings – is sung every year at the Passover table. I was troubled by their large eyes and baleful stare, and was half afraid of them. In essence the goat was regarded as a poor man's cow, though some kept an actual cow.

Nearly everyone kept chickens. We had a few ourselves who scratched around in the street outside, or pecked away at meal times under the kitchen table, and as all chickens felt free to roam as they pleased there were sometimes disputes between neighbours as to whose chicken was whose.

Bashke Ratz claimed she could recognize her fowl better than her own children. She also had a magnificent cock who sired most of the chicks in the neighbourhood, though I don't know if she charged a stud fee.

Though I was rarely required to lift a finger in the house, I had any number of tasks outside it and one of them was overseer of chickens and collector of eggs, which too could lead to disputes. Sometimes I chanced upon an egg in no-man's-land which I thought was ours and Bashke, who believed she could also tell egg from egg, thought was hers.

We didn't have many chickens so that I knew one from the other, and some of them had distinct colouring and very distinct personalities and I suffered deep traumas every time one of them was passed on to father before being prepared for the pot.

The most painful day of the year was thus the eve of Yom Kippur when, as part of an expiation rite, we would grab a chicken, squawking and struggling, by the wings, swing it three times round our heads, and utter the prayer: 'This is my substitute, my vicarious offering, my atonement. This fowl will meet death, but I shall find a long and pleasant life of peace.' After which, according to tradition, one would pass on the chickens to the poor, but the doomed chickens far outnumbered paupers and, laden with our sins though they were, we ate them ourselves – and they didn't taste the worse for it.

It was a gruesome rite based on sheer superstition and we abandoned it once we moved to Glasgow but by then we were chickenless in any case.

No Jewish house in Barovke had dogs, but everyone had cats because everyone had mice, and cats were cheaper than mouse-traps and more effective.

We had several cats. Mother disapproved of them because I would half starve myself to keep them fed, and father because I spent too much time with them.

'*Do vestu khapu a kats in kop,*' he would warn me, you will catch a cat in your head, meaning that my memory would be impaired. In fact I had an uncommonly sound memory as a child, and if I now have some difficulty in recalling recent events, I have no trouble with distant ones.

The problem with cats is that they kept having kittens, usually in my bed, and when I moved them elsewhere, the mother would patiently bring them all back, one by one by the scruff of the neck, and my sisters and I spent half our lives finding homes for them.

Boruch Sholem had what was known as a 'miracle cat', a vast tabby with a spotless dickey and a red collar with a silver bell, who remained resolutely kittenless. She had, of course, been treated by the vet, which was a luxury we could not contemplate.

Barovke was a hard-working community, but the men worked rather less hard than the women, and every Tuesday afternoon some ten to twelve of them would forgather behind drawn curtains round Shmuel Trupin's dining-room table for a game of poker. Father referred to them ironically as the khevra shas, meaning a Talmud study group, though in more irate moments he would denounce them as a *moshav leitzim*, a community of scoffers.

Card-playing was not actually prohibited in Jewish law, but it was strongly discouraged, not only because it involved gambling but because it was *bitul z'man*, a waste of time.

There were far worse sins which one could commit, and far worse sins were committed, but furtively. The *yozhniks*, as father called them, committed theirs blatantly, and their drawn curtains did not so much hide the transgression as proclaim it.

It was bad enough to be a *kartchosnick* oneself, it was infinitely worse to provide a venue for other *kartchosnicks*. It made Trupin's house a place of low resort.

People in Barovke locked and bolted their doors last thing at night, but during daylight hours we felt free to wander in and out of each other's homes, and I would sometimes stand and watch Shmuel and his crowd with bewilderment, for they sat half-hidden in smoke, silent and intent, with small stacks of coins amid overflowing ashtrays. It didn't seem much fun. Father's khevra shas didn't seem much fun either, but at least they were performing a *mitzva*, and religious duties didn't have to be fun. Indeed, as I already knew from my own experience, they usually weren't.

As I mentioned, father gave five or six sermons a year and at least one of them included a mandatory denunciation of *kartchosnicks*, without, of course, naming names, but then, given the size of Barovke, he didn't have to. It almost became a ritual. People waited for it, and were disappointed when it didn't come.

He also took the matter up privately with Trupin, who always came up with the same excuse:

'But Reb Azriel, it's not gambling. I always lose. It's my way of giving charity to the poor. As far as *bitul z'man*, what do you expect me to do with my free time, study the Talmud? I'm far too stupid for that.'

But it was not only a matter of cards. Father made a point of ignoring gossip on his principle of, 'if I haven't seen it, it hasn't happened', but even he could not overlook the mildly libidinous air about the entire Trupin establishment. There was first of all his wife Soreleh, the divorcee – rare in Latvia, let alone Barovke – and a thoroughly attractive one at that, and if one passed the place in the evening there was often the sound of ribald laughter. People were having fun, which in itself carried ominous overtones of sin. Father may not have been a puritan by nature, but as a graduate of Slobodka he was a puritan by training.

'One day I'm going to take his kosher licence away,' he kept saying, to which he would add despairingly, 'the trouble is I can't get angry with Shmuel. Nobody can.'

I noticed as we worked our way through Scripture during our daily lessons that father lingered over some passages and skated over others, as if my awareness of certain human functions and habits might impair my development, and when I felt moved by curiosity or bewilderment to pull him up he could get impatient and testy.

Thus, for example, when we came to Leviticus 15:19: 'And if a woman have an issue, and the issue in her flesh be blood, she shall be in her impurity seven days ...' I wanted further and better particulars.

'She was bleeding,' said father, 'anyone can bleed.'

'But why should she be unclean for seven days?'

'Because it was unclean blood. Now let's get on with it.'

There was a local midwife – an *akusherke* – who was a government employee. She was a short Latvian woman with pince-nez and wore a navy-blue uniform with a silver badge in her hat. She went everywhere on foot, with a bulging leather bag in her hand, and had a brisk, purposeful walk, as if always in a hurry, which she probably was.

There was a man in Barovke known as Hershel der heyker – Hershel the hunchback – to distinguish him from the several Hershels who were not hunchbacks. There were also any number of women whom I thought of as hunch-fronts but while Hershel's hump was permanent, theirs subsided after a visit from the midwife, and until I was seven or eight I presumed that a midwife was some sort of hump-doctor and wondered why she never attempted to treat poor Hershel. I did, however, notice that after she left a house there was always the harsh cry of an infant. Until I was eight I thought that she brought them in her bag. I never even tried to work out where she could have got them in the first place. I was a backward child.

I was not, however, totally ignorant because later – thanks to Leipkaleh – I knew that it took a man and a woman to have a child, but that if anything, added to my bewilderment, for there was a dressmaker in Barovke who had a daughter and grand-daughter living with her, and though there were seven or eight cats in the household, a well as a parrot, there wasn't a single man. I asked father why.

'He's dead,' he said, which was his favourite way of closing a conversation.

Chapter 7

Solemn and Festive

Jewish life in Barovke was dominated by the festivals, the most important of which were the Yomim Neroim, the Solemn Days, also known as the High Holy Days, which consist of Rosh Hashonoh (the New Year) and Yom Kippur (the Day of Atonement).

New Year, in the west certainly, is regarded as part of, if not the climax to, the whoopee season. Among devout Jews it is a time for soul-searching and contrition, and one prepared for the event by assembling in synagogue some days before the actual festival for breast-beating and penitential prayers (*selichos*) at the crack of dawn.

Few people in Barovke had clocks and those who did were not disposed to be in synagogue at dawn, and Moishe Yudeh, who looked as if he never slept at all, was the local knocker-upper. He would go round the village with a long stick, rap on the shutters and cry out in his plaintive croak: '*Shtayt oyf tzu slikhes!*' The very sound of his voice conveyed the solemnity of the season.

Young and old would answer his call and within minutes the streets of the village were filled with muffled figures, lanterns in hand, making their way slowly to synagogue through the swirling mists of early autumn.

Tishrei, the first Jewish month, generally coincides with October. The skies were darker, the days shorter and there was already a hint of winter in the air, which in itself induced a mood of contrition, and though I was not, as yet, much of a sinner, I had enough on my conscience to join enthusiastically in the prayers: 'Be gracious to us, our Father, for we have sinned. Forgive us our King, for we have strayed, for thou art our Lord, good and forgiving ... '

And at the end of the service father would sound a blast on the *shofar* – of which he was a virtuoso – long, shrill, eerie and laden with doom to warn us what lay ahead if we failed to mend our ways.

The *selichos* were, in essence, a softening-up process, to make God more disposed to forgive, and make his chosen more worthy of forgiveness, to draw them away from the material world in which they were immersed and bring them nearer the *malchus shomayim*, the Kingdom of Heaven. And it must be said that the very effort of rising at dawn induced a passing sense of virtue even in someone of my age, even if I slept through much of the service.

If these were the mere preliminaries to Rosh Hahonoh and Yom Kippur, one can imagine the solemnities which attached to the days themselves, and yet I loved most of the ceremonies associated with them, the singing, the prayers, the ready company provided by the crowded synagogues, the sense of occasion, the splendid fare at home, the sight of Barovke in its festive gear. As far as I was concerned they were happy rather than solemn days, even if they were accompanied by tension within our household.

Mother not only had an endless succession of meals to prepare, but had to prepare herself, for women were expected to be in synagogue on the High Festivals and as queen of Barovke she had to be decently attired. Not that she could allow herself to be poorly attired at other times of the year, but during the High Festival she was on formal display, as were her daughters, and as she could rarely afford new clothes she had to restyle the old ones, unstitching and restitching, cutting away a piece here, adding a piece there. She, of course, began well before the festivals, but accelerated as they drew near, rushing from stove to sewing machine, from sewing machine to stove, with pins in her mouth and murder in her heart.

She was, as I shall show, even worse as Passover drew near, and much as I loved the festivals I came to loathe the approaches to them.

It was also the most fraught time of the year for father. He had whole herds of cattle and sheep and whole flocks of poultry to slaughter. He also had a complete cycle of sermons to prepare and he agitated and cogitated over every word he uttered. He would go through half his library in the course of preparations, consulting one volume, making notes from another, absorbing a third, and rehearsing memorable phrases, some from the texts, others of his own invention. He even rehearsed his gestures, for though he was widely liked and highly regarded he did not take such matters for granted and was, so to speak, on trial not only in the sight of God but in the eyes of man.

He inevitably built his sermons round the theme of forgiveness and would explain that if we expected God to forgive us, we must be prepared to forgive others and to purge ourselves of any sense of resentment, ill feeling or envy, but while he lived up to his teachings at other times of the year, he was not always capable of doing so once the High Holy Days approached.

As I have said, father functioned as rabbi, teacher, *shochet* and *khazan* (cantor). He had a pleasant singing voice, and was not only familiar with all the traditional melodies, but with every line of the liturgy, their hidden meanings, and the events which had inspired them, so that he prayed with sincerity and feeling. He was, however, incapable of fancy trills and bravura displays, and once the festivals approached, the elders of Barovke would secure the services of a professional cantor.

It was the same every year and every year Beirach would be delegated to break the news to father. In fact father knew his recital off by heart.

'It's not as if we don't appreciate your singing, Reb Azriel, because as you well know, we love it, and as I always tell my wife, you're worth any ten *hazonim*. But we mustn't expect too much of one man. This is a busy time of the year for you and you work from morning till night. The services are long, you'd have to be on your feet all day and even you, Reb Azriel, also deserve a rest.'

But father was not interested in a rest. For all his humility he had an exhibitionist streak and liked an audience, preferably a large one. He was assured one for his sermons, but did not care to be upstaged by the cantor, and upstaged he was if only because the cantor was an import.

What made it worse was the fact that the so-called professionals were, in his eyes, not all that professional. He often said that he would go to the ends of the earth to hear a good cantor. He had heard the great Sirota in Warsaw and said it was one of the most memorable experiences of his life, but he resented the sort of *chazonim* who surfaced in Barovke, '*oysgeklapte hoyshanos*', as he called them, clapped-out hacks, who couldn't sing, garbled their Hebrew and desecrated God's name every time they opened their mouths.

Given the sort of fees Barovke could afford it could only attract old men – sometimes very old men – at the end of their careers, or very young men at the beginning of theirs, and father resented the latter even more than the former.

'They can sing,' he said, 'but they can't read.' They also lacked the gravitas the occasion demanded and some of them were even beardless.

The liturgy was sombre:

'On the New Year it is inscribed, and on the Day of Atonement it will be sealed ... who shall live and who shall die, who in the fullness of his years and who before it, who shall perish by fire and who by water, who by the sword, who by wild beasts, who by hunger and who by thirst; who by earthquake and who by plague, who by strangling and who by stoning ... who shall be at ease and who afflicted, who shall be poor and who will wax rich, who shall be brought low, and who exalted.'

Father, even within the limited range of his voice could evoke the full portent of the language, while the cantor romped through it as if were a ditty, or worse, treated it as an aria.

And finally a cantor was a *klei-kodesh*, a holy vessel, a clergyman of sorts, and having two clergymen in one synagogue was like having two women in one kitchen.

What added to the irony of the occasion was that whoever the cantor, and however his performance, father had to invite the man home to a meal on Rosh Hashonoh and, as a courtesy, would ask him to perform at table, and he would not need much asking.

The sort of cantors who came to Barovke were never asked back a second time, or never cared to come back. The only exception was a man called Birnbaum, a large, slow-moving, shaggy figure, like a hobbled buffalo, with a voice to match, who had handkerchiefs in every pocket to wipe the sweat which kept pouring from him even at mealtimes.

When father asked him for a *niggun*, he sucked his teeth, cleared his throat, pinged his tuning fork on a glass, sat back, grasped the table to steady himself, and the rafters quivered, and the windows rattled as he let go.

Our neighbours, Chaim Ratz, his wife, his son, his daughter-in-law and their two children, left their tables and rapped on our windows, so that they could also listen.

A *nigun* means a tune, a melody. What we were offered was something like a grand opera and by the time he finished half of Barovke was crowded round our house.

I was fascinated, not so much by the singer or his songs, as by the rivers of sweat which poured down his face, accumulated in his beard, and dropped in steady blobs on the tablecloth.

Yom Kippur, which follows about a week after Rosh Hashonoh, is the high point of the Jewish year and the most solemn day in the Jewish calendar.

It was the one day – actually a night and a day – when everyone came to synagogue, including even those absolved from all religious obligation at other times of the year – Pinchashowits the engineer, Heller the doctor, Hurwitz the dentist and Krochmal the apothecary. And their wives too, Mrs Heller, Mrs Hurwitz and Mrs Krochmal, in elegant hats and Riga finery.

Mrs Pinchashowits, a tall, slender, handsome woman, with huge luminous eyes, was more austerely dressed in a beret and a simple blouse and skirt. I suspect she disliked ostentation and did not want to upstage or outshine the women around her. If so her motives were misunderstood.

'I know she thinks we're peasants,' said mother, 'but you'd think on Yom Kippur at least she would take the trouble to look decent. If she has no respect for man, she should at least have respect for God.'

Father was dressed in a *kittel* for the occasion, a white gown which mother starched so thoroughly that it was almost like a suit of armour, and which crackled as he moved. The other officiants were similarly attired as were some of the elders including Beirach, Boruch Sholem, Shimshon Ber and, rather surprisingly, the Cossack, Binyomin Rosin. The cover over the reading desk was in white and gold, as was the cover over the ark.

There was always considerable commotion both upstairs and downstairs as one waited for Kol Nidrei, the opening service, to begin. People who may not have seen each other for as long as a week, shook hands and exchanged greetings, or pushed through the throng to get to their seats, but once the cantor rose to his feet, cleared his throat, and pinged his fork, an expectant hush descended on the congregation.

The actual prayers with which the service opens and which are accompanied by a great deal of pomp and ceremony can be finished in a minute, and are immediately followed by the sermon. No cantor, however, took less than ten and some, by dint of repetition took as long as half an hour, and father – being the next act – had to summon all his patience not to tell him to get on with it.

Father was no hell-fire preacher for Jews don't believe in hell, in so far as they do, they presume that it is to be experienced right here on earth, and father went in for worldly sermons, and was cerebral rather than emotional, though he liked to embellish his remarks with numerous legends.

One of his teachers at Slobodka had told him that everything he would ever need for a sermon could be found in one line of Micah: 'What doth the Lord want of thee, but to do justly, love mercy and walk humbly with thy God.'

He looked impressive with his *tallith* drawn over his head, his white garb, long beard, dark eyes and handsome features, and he spoke with clarity, force and conviction. Heads on every side would nod with approval, and though I was not in a position to assess his performance, I noticed that no one slept, which, given the sort of meals people had before the fast, was no small feat, but he never spoke for long.

'There is only one rule to preaching,' he said, 'stop before they've had enough – which sometimes means that you shouldn't even start.'

Though father had great affection for his congregation he sometimes felt – and mother always did – that his sermons deserved a more sophisticated audience, and on Yom Kippur he found one, for there in the front row were Pinchashowits, Heller, Hurwitz and Krochmal.

Although – or because – he had not been to university himself, father had great awe for lettered men, people who enjoyed standing not only among Jews, but among non-Jews, and he would address himself principally to them. I am not even sure if they all understood Yiddish – Dr Heller almost certainly did not – but they all listened intently and Pinchashowits always made a point of congratulating him on his delivery and content. What diminished father's pleasure was the fact that he also made a point of congratulating the cantor.

On Yom Kippur we spent the entire day in synagogue, and all the adults fasted. Small children, of course, were not expected to fast at all and those from about ten to 13 years fasted till lunchtime. The competitive spirit, however, entered into even Yom Kippur. Zamke Zussman who was then nine or ten, claimed that he could fast longer than any of us.

I was never agile and could not run as fast or jump as high as the others, or climb as far in the steam room as Zamke, but when it came to fasting I thought I could hold my own, and most of the gang also rose to the challenge.

Shaike gave up by lunchtime, which made it difficult for the rest of us for we could imagine him nibbling drumsticks and drinking *zeltser*. By two Welfke and Shmulik dropped out. By three I was beginning to wilt, though Zamke was still going strong, but then about an hour later when we went out for an airing, the rush of fresh air suddenly went to my head and I keeled over.

Zamke promptly revived me with a glass of water and I rushed home for a bite in case my parents should hear about it. In fact mother had heard about it and arrived breathless and ashen faced just as I was sinking my teeth into an apple. If it hadn't been Yom Kippur she would have killed me.

Father was in high spirits at the end of the day, even before he broke his fast, and was in higher spirits after, for he always broke it on herrings and vodka. The tensions were over, the cantor was leaving or about to leave, he would have Barovke to himself.

But there was also a general feeling that we had all, young and old, purged our sins. 'We now have a clean sheet,' father would say, which was a reassuring thought, for by the age of eight I had a fairly stained one, and I sometimes wondered if the delinquencies to which I later succumbed were due to an ingrained belief in divine forgiveness.

Succoth, the Feast of Tabernacles which followed five days after Yom Kippur, was sheer joy. The event commemorates the wandering of the Israelites in the wilderness, and every household in Barovke built a small *succah* – a booth covered with foliage in which the males of the family ate throughout the seven days of the festival.

Women were not actually barred from the *succah*, but they were under no obligation to use it and in our family, certainly, they preferred not to, for it could be cold in October, especially at night, and we ate in coats and mufflers.

My mother and sisters served the meals, and cleared away the dishes, but otherwise stayed indoors.

We usually had at least one visitor to our main meals, and sometimes two or three. The cramped conditions and the discomfort somehow added to the chumminess of the gatherings, and so in a strange way did the absence of womenfolk. Women, young or old, would have represented a worldly intrusion upon an unworldly event. They could never enter fully into the spirit of the occasion; they weren't trained to do so and if anything were discouraged from doing so.

I also noticed that they cramped father's style. He was more relaxed and at ease among men, and more prolix. There would always be a bottle of schnapps on the table, vodka, or *zeks un nayntsiker*, 96%-proof spirit which was almost pure alcohol and smelt like the fuel we used on our primus stove, and for all I know it may have been primus-stove fuel. Some of our guests arrived with something even stronger, and when a drop spilled over it burned a hole in the tablecloth.

Father enjoyed a drink at any time but when the occasion was religious he enjoyed it religiously, and once he and his guests had knocked back a glass or two, the singing would begin, not so much songs, as *nigunim*, or wordless hymns, with clapping of hands, snapping of fingers and swaying and aying, and all with such vigour that the cold was forgotten.

And finally once Succoth was over came the merriest event of all, Simchas Torah, which is the culmination of the entire cycle of festivals, and a compensation for all the solemnity surrounding Roh Hashonoh and Yom Kippur, both of which were concerned with atonement and forgiveness. By Simchas Torah one had been forgiven – or one presumed one had. If one hadn't it was too late to do anything about it, which was all the more reason to drink, though the festival itself was connected with quite another event.

A portion of the Pentateuch, as the five books of Moses are known, is read every week, the entire cycle being completed and resumed anew on Simchas Torah. The Torah scrolls were at the centre of the celebrations and were carried round the synagogue seven times to prolonged singing and dancing. Women can only act as observers but in Barovke they would descend from their galleries to observe the events more closely, to join in the singing and clapping and to scatter sweets among the children. Father, as rabbi, was master of revels, and he entered whole-heartedly into the spirit of the occasions.

There was vodka almost on tap throughout a good part of the morning service, and there would be more drinking in different homes once the service was over. Everyone insisted on having father as guest, and father was perfectly happy to accept. Mother was rather less happy about it and would pull him in one direction, while his prospective hosts, themselves mildly inebriated, would pull in another, and they generally won. In October 1937, on his last Simchas Torah in Barovke, father nearly drank himself to death.

He had managed to stagger home leaning heavily on mother's arm, had something to eat, and immediately dropped off to sleep.

A few hours later he was seized with convulsive pains. I was alone with him in the house and ran to tell mother. She arrived breathlessly, took one look at him and sent me to call Dr Heller.

Heller lived some distance away on the outskirts of Barovke. His house was in darkness without any sign of life and a neighbour told me he was away and wouldn't be back till the next day.

In the meantime, father having failed to appear for evening service in synagogue, the synagogue came to our house, and when I got back people were milling around everywhere. Boruch Sholem was trying to give father a drink, but he kept bringing it up, and was still writhing with agony. I told mother Heller wasn't in town, and she threw up her hands.

'God, God, what shall I do, what shall I do?'

Most alarming of all, old Moishe Yudeh, who adored father, was chanting Psalms – the Jewish equivalent of extreme unction – in a corner with tears streaming down his face.

Some minutes later Abrasha Pinchashowits pulled up in his car, and when he heard that Heller wasn't available he drove off to get another doctor from a nearby town.

Mother ordered me to bed and I went to my little alcove, undressed, washed, said my bedtime prayer, and settled into sleep, resigned to the thought that when I woke I would be an orphan.

When I woke the next morning, however, father was there beside me, smiling cheerfully, and I thought it had all been a dream.

Pinchashovits had returned with a doctor who promptly applied a stomach pump, and father was cured within minutes, but by then mother was on the point of collapse.

While the Tishrei cycle of festivals lasted, we virtually lived in synagogue and I was rarely out of my festive gear. Once they were over it was like facing the workaday world after a very prolonged Sabbath. It meant workaday clothes and workaday food, school and homework, a certain amount of harassment in the classroom, a certain amount of bullying in the playground, a lack of cheer all round. I felt secure in the world of the synagogue, vulnerable in the world outside, and there were no immediate festivals to anticipate.

There were none at all in Kheshvan, the second month of the year, and the only happy event in prospect was Chanukah, or the festival of lights, which comes towards the end of December and often coincides with Christmas.

The Tishrei cycle of festivals, Passover and Pentecost are all very ancient and derive from Scripture. Chanukah, in Jewish terms, is comparatively recent and commemorates a successful Jewish revolt against their Greek overlords in the second century BC. Jewish victories were fairly rare so that it was something to celebrate but, though Chanukah lasts eight days, it is a minor festival. There are extra prayers, but no special services in synagogue, no festive meals, and no festive gear which, as far as I was concerned, was a major drawback.

Though shy and retiring in some respects, I was an exhibitionist in others and liked to be seen in my fancy best. The clothes I wore on weekdays were made by my mother, usually out of clothes previously worn by my father or even my sisters, though mother could work wonders with her sewing machine, men's wear was not her forte and I looked like a *shloch* and felt like one.

When I was younger I used to wear a sailor suit – of the type favoured by the Tsar's children – on the Sabbath and festivals, but from about the age of eight I wore a suit made by Chaim Ratz, a shirt bought from Moishe Zeitlin, and machine-made brown leather sandals which had come all the way from Dvinsk.

I was still not quite the picture of elegance, for I had thin legs and, no matter how tight my garters, I found it difficult to keep my socks up, but even then I felt taller, more erect, more self-confident, a *mensch*, and if I did not dress as well as Shaike Trupin, I looked infinitely better than Zamke, Shmulik, Welfke and the rest of the gang and my sisters' friends would refer to me as *der kreshavits* – the handsome one. A festival which left me in my workaday clothes, therefore, was a very minor one in my eyes, but Chanukah did have its attractions.

First of all there were the lights themselves. Every male in the household had his own *menorah*, a candelabrum with eight branches, and we would light one candle on the first night, two on the second until, on the last night of Chanukah, all eight were lit and one could see them flickering in every window in Barovke and reflected in the snow.

Chatzkal-with-the-six-sons had 56 candles blazing away on the last night of Chanukah. It was bright and warm in his house, but almost impossible to breathe.

The lighting-up ceremony was accompanied by special songs and there would be a distribution of Chanukah *gelt* – Chanukah money – and it was about the only time of the year when I had actual cash jingling in my pockets.

There was no Heder on Chanukah, which was a joy in its own right, but there was an annual Heder treat which was less than a joy, for it was always accompanied by speeches.

Speeches were the bane of Jewish life – as to an extent they still are – for whatever the occasion, whether grave or gay, there was always someone around who felt compelled to say 'a few words', except that they were never few. Father often made speeches, but they were part of his job and he was paid to do so, but I could never understand why people who were perfectly at liberty to stay silent, and who had nothing to say, chose to say it.

We sometimes had visiting speakers on Chanukah from out of town, invariably billed as *der bavuste reyder* – the well-known orator – well-known being the Yiddish euphemism for unknown. They were usually Zionists and they would speak about events in Palestine, and even though they spoke at great length and could still be boring, we sensed that we were at least being bored in a good cause.

We still had school on Chanukah, but school, as the year drew to a close, had its compensations, for classrooms were decorated with streamers and bunting and a huge fir tree was installed in the school hall in preparation for Christmas.

We had two Christmases, the Lutheran one, celebrated in school itself on 25 December, and the Russian Orthodox one, celebrated in the village on 6 January. There were lights everywhere, and processions and carols and a generous distribution of sweets but, thankfully, no speeches. In fact Chanukah blended in my imagination with the two Christmases. I joined enthusiastically in all three and sang the Christmas carols as lustily as the Chanukah songs (though not within the hearing of my father). I was game for any celebrations going.

Barovke was by then half buried in snow and almost inaccessible to the outside world and Chanukah and the two Christmases helped to compensate for the descent of winter.

Chanukah was followed by two fairly blank months in which there were hardly any celebrations at all, but then in the month of Adar, which corresponds roughly to March, came the minor Festival of Purim which also celebrates the Jews' triumph over their enemies but, while the events surrounding Chanukah took place in the Jewish homeland, the events surrounding Purim took place in ancient Persia.

Purim usually coincided with the local pre-lenten carnivals though the festive spirit which affected both Jew and Gentile may have been due more to the change of season than the demands of tradition.

The grip of winter had begun to ease by then, the air had softened, snows were melting, the forests were losing their white canopy, patches of green were appearing everywhere and young and old were of a mood to celebrate the end of their long hibernation.

The story of Purim, as told in the Book of Esther, is like something out of the *Arabian Nights* and has most of the components of a fairy story: a comical king, Ahasuerus; a wicked vizier, Haman; a beautiful queen Esther, who unbeknown to the king, is Jewish; her cousin Mordechai, a courtier. Haman comes to resent the influence of Mordechai and the prosperity of the Jews and draws up a plot to destroy them all. Whereupon Esther reveals her origin and foils his plot, and the king allows the Jews to arm themselves and destroy their enemies.

It all sounds a little improbable and there is no external

evidence to suggest that the people mentioned ever existed or that the events described ever took place, but no believing Jew has any need for external evidence to back up the claims of Scripture. As far as we were concerned, we were celebrating a great historical event and did so with shrill exuberance and great enthusiasm.

We would arrive in synagogue in fancy dress. My sisters took my transformation in hand and I usually came with blackened features, a turban and false beard and could have passed for Ahasuerus, Mordechai Haman or even Ali Baba. Girls also joined in the fun and came invariably as Esthers, and instead of ascending to the ladies' gallery, would mill around downstairs with the boys while father read out the Book of Esther.

Haman, until the rise of Hitler, symbolized the arch enemy of the Jews, though a stranger to the synagogue might have taken him for the hero of the story, for every time his name was mentioned there would be loud whoops, whistles, the clapping of wooden clappers (specially made for the event) and the rattling of rattles. Older boys detonated corks stuffed with gunpowder and by the end of the evening the congregation was half lost in a cloud of cordite and the synagogue smelt like a battlefield.

The next morning people would exchange gifts, usually edibles, and as we received gifts from everyone and had to reciprocate we spent hours repacking our presents and passing them on. It was a fairly universal practice, and the same packet of nuts and raisins could pass through 20 or 30 hands, before ending up with the original sender.

One was actually enjoined to drink and get drunk on Purim. We wouldn't touch the vodka and spirits favoured by our elders, which smelt like poison and tasted like poison and which, imbibed in any quantity, was poisonous, but Zamke Zussman's mother made a fairly potent brew out of cherries and sugar which she called 'brendy'. It went well with the *homentashen*, the triangular poppy-seed cakes, specially baked for Purim, and we would come away from her house feeling pleasantly befuddled.

Once Purim was over, Passover was in sight, and though I loved the festival itself, I regarded the approaches to it with a certain amount of dread – as I still do.

Passover was, and is, an expensive occasion, and once Purim was over father would meet with Boruch Sholem, Shmuel Trupin and Beirach to make sure that everyone had the necessary wherewithal to celebrate the event.

Of the 40 or so families in Barovke perhaps as many as ten were in need, but none of them had to apply for help because everyone knew how much everyone was worth, or, more particularly wasn't. Needs were carefully assessed and father was delegated to deliver the largesse by way of a social call.

Matzo was baked locally in ovens specially prepared for the purpose, and father supervised every stage of the process to make sure that not even a microscopic trace of *chomets* – leavening – fell into the dough. He wore white overalls and covered his head with a tight white cap, as did everyone else, but his beard must have been a *chomets*-trap.

It was a complex operation. Everything – the mixing, the kneading, the drawing, the perforating, the cutting, the packing – was done by hand, and there were about a dozen people involved.

Every household had a vast wickerwork basket in which it would store enough *matzos* to see it through the entire eight days of the festival, and father would inspect every basket to make sure that it too was free of *chomets*.

I generally liked to poke my nose into everything, but this was the one time of the year when I was careful to keep out of father's way, for father the manager and supervisor, was a different person from father the rabbi and teacher, and was impatient, testy and on edge. Mother was even worse.

As I may have suggested, mother was not particularly house-proud but once Passover drew near she would not so much clean the house as attack it. She would batten down her hair under a tight kerchief, tighten her lips, roll up her sleeves, don a new apron, launch her attack like a whirling dervish on the attic and would not rest until she had worked her way down to the cellar and, indeed, through the cellar.

The whole operation took nearly a month. She had Anna to help her, and my sisters also gave a hand as soon as they were home from school.

Mother in top gear was a terrifying sight. Father and I tried to keep out of her way, and I was ready to suffer hunger and thirst if only to avoid the clouds of dust and shrieks of fury which accompanied her progress, but we were conscripted to move the furniture, and coins, brooches, safety-pins, hairpins, powderpuffs, liptstick holders, cough lozenges, pencils, pens, knick-knacks which had been given up for lost suddenly reappeared. Everything washable was washed, everything scrubbable was scrubbed and not a speck of dust was suffered to remain in place.

Then on the eve of the festival father and I would move all the pots and pans, cutlery and crockery used during the year up to the attic, and would bring the crockery and cutlery and the pots and pans, used only on Passover, down. It was a delicate and lengthy operation, for our ladder – as everything else in the house – was rickety but I enjoyed every minute of it, for it meant that the annual catharsis was over.

And then in the evening when everything glowed and gleamed and the house was a showplace, mother collapsed in a heap and spent half the festival in bed.

Passover opens with a ceremony called the *seder*, which is part service and part banquet, and a child in the family – preferably a male child, though females are not actually barred from doing so – launches proceedings by asking four questions, all of them rather banal. The point of it all is to hold the attention and excite the curiosity of the young, and by way of reply the head of the household reads through the Hagadah which, with extracts from Scripture, gives the early history of the Jewish people right through the exodus from Egypt.

As the only son of the family, I was of course the questioner and I loved the occasion because I loved the attention. There were six of us in the family and even with mother in bed we always had guests, Shimshon Ber and his daughter, Moshe Yudeh and his wife, der Alter Bock and his mother, and any stray soul so unfortunate as to be stranded in Barovke over Passover. In other words I had an audience and a fairly large one, and revelled in the approving glances I received on every side.

One had to drink four large cups of wine in the course of the proceedings. Real wine, which came from Palestine via London, was an unheard-of luxury. Father had a bottle – an annual gift from Boruch Sholem – which he shared with me and the other menfolk. The womenfolk drank mead, which was fairly dreadful, like a flat, stale, muddy beer.

The meal which followed was, however, superb, course after course of mother's splendid cuisine. Stuffed pike with horseradish; a golden chicken soup with *matzo* dumplings; roast chicken with roast potatoes, parsnips and carrots. The inevitable stewed apple and prunes which came at the end were something of an anticlimax but were still enjoyed.

Finally, there came the ceremony of the *afikomon* which over the years became a source of distress to me.

The *afikomon* – half a piece of *matzo* – is hidden at the beginning of the evening by the head of the household in order to retain the attention of the children, and whoever finds it at the end can demand a present from his father before he surrenders it.

I always found it and always demanded a bicycle, and father always promised to get me one, but never said when. I finally got it when I was *bar mitzvah* – but even then it was secondhand.

In synagogue the next morning, the inevitable question was who had the longest *seder*.

'Finished at 11,' said Shaike.

'Midnight,' claimed Zamke.

I was able to trump them all because we rarely finished before one, and when they refused to believe me I had any number of witnesses to prove it.

The joy of Passover came not only with the events we were commemorating and the many ceremonies they entailed but with the season. It was spring, but even spring had its drawbacks.

If Chanukah coincided with Christmas, Passover coincided with Easter, and while I could join happily in the one, the other was another matter. I was not sure what it was all about but I was vaguely aware that it was to the Gentiles what Yom Kippur was to the Jews. They dressed in their best, spent long hours in church, and there was nothing boisterous or colourful to their celebration other than the exchange of brightly painted eggs.

It was also, according to Jewish lore, a time of the year when non-Jews turned nasty and accused Jews of abducting young children to use their blood in their *matzo*. It was the beginning of the pogrom season.

I am not aware that there was ever a blood libel case in Latvia, and there were certainly no pogroms until the Nazi invasion in 1941, but Jewish attitudes are often shaped by past events, rather than present realities, and the Gentiles did look less friendly and more distant, and there was a sense of unease in Barovke throughout the four days of the festival.

At about the same time, there was an annual visitation which afflicted us all, the great thaw which began slowly in March and accelerated in the course of April.

With the exception of the tarmacked highway to Dvinsk, the roads in and around Barovke were dirt tracks and once the snows melted they turned to quagmires, and even the highway was often flooded. We were cut off for days on end and there were occasions when the Thursday market – the highpoint of the week, and on which much of Barovke depended for its livelihood – was cancelled.

There were two private cars in Barovke, one owned by Pinchashowits, the other by the midwife's husband. (We didn't know what he did for a living, and presumed that owning a car was in itself a livelihood.) They too got bogged down when they tried to venture out, and we were spattered with mud as we tried to push them clear.

Mud, in fact, was as much a part of spring as snow was of winter, and about the only safe way of getting around was on horseback, which was not an option available to many Jews in Barovke.

But whatever the drawbacks of spring, it always carried the promise of summer, and in the summer Barovke came into its own.

Chapter 8

Left Ones and Free Ones

We lived in a small enclosed world but the enclosure was self-imposed. Latvian Jews, who formed some of the population, were not subject to any restrictions and if they tended to stick together in large or small close-knit communities it was because they wanted to be within easy reach of a synagogue, a Heder, a Jewish cemetery, a kosher butcher, grocer, baker. Their ceremonies and traditions called for a ghetto, but even where they no longer adhered to God, they still tended to adhere to each other. They no longer felt menaced by non-Jews, but were more at ease with one another.

There were two Yiddish words which I heard rather often and which sounded so alike that I tended to confuse them and when I asked father the difference between them, he said, '*Eyne iz erger vi di andere,*' one is worse than the other, which didn't tell me much.

The words were *gesamt* and *geshmadt*. The one meant poisoned and the other converted. Both represented ultimate tragedies, Jews who could no longer bear life at all, or could no longer bear to be Jewish. Where a person took poison, however, he only gave up his life, but if he converted, he not only gave up his soul, worse, he betrayed his people.

Father used to play on the similarity between the expressions to suggest that where one began with the poison of alien culture one ended with abjuring one's faith and he rarely missed an opportunity to berate, '*di linke, di fraye, and di asimilatorn*' – the left ones, the free ones and the assimilated ones, all of whom, in his eyes, were much of a muchness, and all of whom felt in one way or another that Judaism did not meet their needs, which is no doubt why he regarded his own home town of Kreslavka as *treyf* (non-Jew, non-kosher). It was dominated by *linke* and *fraye*.

There were no such Jews in Barovke, he would proudly claim, but the fact that the word *frei*, meaning free, was a term of opprobrium in his eyes, said everything about the sort of attitudes he had imbibed, for he felt that no decent man, and certainly no decent Jew, would want, or should want, to be completely free.

He liked to tell the story of how he was once summoned to a remote hamlet to the bed of a dying man, whom he had never seen in synagogue, who never believed in anything, and who had never lived like a Jew, but who wanted to be buried as one. It was a touching story and he told it well, even if he told it often, but I was never quite sure what point he was trying to make.

Father was a prisoner of his training and whatever benefits he may have received from his years in the *yeshiva*, a critical faculty was not one of them. He was brought up to believe that the only culture which counted was Jewish culture and that everything else, even if superficially attractive, was false or, at best, frivolous, but then he was never really exposed to anything else. Though bookish, he never picked up a Russian book and never read a page of Tolstoy, Dostoevsky or Pushkin. It was something that he read the Yiddish classics, but was rather furtive about it for some of them verged on the heretical. Rather surprisingly, he was familiar with some of Shakespeare's plays, which he read in a Hebrew translation from the Russian, but never witnessed an actual performance in any language, for he never set foot in the theatre and, as far as I know, the only time he went to the cinema was to see a film about Dachau.

Every Chanukah he spoke about the Maccabees who had not only risen against their Greek overlords, but against Jews who had

turned to Greek culture. And as Passover approached, he would
recall that the Israelites had been redeemed from bondage in
Egypt because they were true to themelves; they had never
changed their names, or their culture, and didn't even speak
Arabic, unlike *die linke die frie* and *die assimilatorn*, who were
turning to other cultures and were betraying themselves.

Father made few sermons but many speeches and he invoked
die linke, die frie and *die assimilatorn* with such regularity that I
came to regard them as a sort of invocation, like the blessing he
made when he consecrated a house. And yet there were the
famous four, Pinchashowits, Heller, Hurwitz and Krochmal, who
represented all three categories and whom father approached with
almost cringing veneration. This was particularly the case with
Pinchashowits, whom he described as *a yid, a tsaddik, ober on
Yiddishkeit* (a saintly Jew, but without Judaism), but never
recognized that there was anything even remotely inconsistent in
his attitude.

'There are always exceptions,' he would say, but even in the
general community once children entered school they applied
themselves to their secular studies with a determination and zeal
they never showed in Heder and father himself was proud of the
knowledge of Latvian displayed by my sisters.

Among my contemporaries, I alone hoped to go on to *yeshiva*
and become a rabbi. Zamke wanted to be a soldier, of all things,
and in the cavalry at that, while most of the others had vague
dreams – no doubt nurtured by their parents – of becoming a
Pinchashowits, a Heller, a Hurwitz or a Krochmal in their own
right.

In later years I began to wonder if father ever had an idea of his
own, or even if he had fully worked out the full implications of the
ideas he received. When faced with some moral dilemma he
would not consult his heart or his mind, but the sacred texts, and
when he had something to say he would almost invariably begin
with, *es shteyt in posek*, meaning it is written in Scripture, or *di
gemore zogt*, the Talmud says, and this applied even to
contemporary events.

'What do you think of Karlis Ulmanis?'

(*above left*) Paternal grandfather Avron Meyer from Kreslavka and his son and stepmother.

(*above right*) Chaim's maternal grandmother and Uncle Oremates.

(*below*) A family gathering in Breslev; back row from left to right: Miriam, Rachmiel, Chaim Kasre's wife, Chaim's mother, Laike, Sonja; middle row: Chaim, Chaim Kasre, Chaim's maternal grandmother, Laike's husband Welfke and their children, Chaim's sister Leba to his right.

(*above left*) Uncle Rachmiel's visit to Barovke; from left to right, Sonja, Leba, Chaim and Miriam. (*above right*) This photograph is thought to have been taken prior to the Bermant family's departure to Glasgow; from left to right: Miriam, Sonja, Chaim and Leba.

(*below*) Chaim in Breslev as a two- or three-year-old.

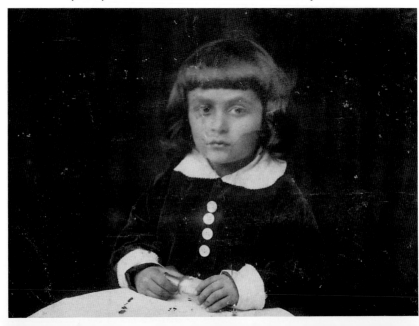

(*above*) Chaim aged seven in Barovke.

(*above*) Reb Azriel Bermant, Chaim's father, as a young man; (*below left*) Chaim's mother as a young woman, and (*below right*) Chaim's mother with his sister Miriam in Dvinsk.

A group of Ha-Shomer Ha-Tzair children in Barovke. The two boys kneeling at either end of the front row are Mendel Fleishman's older brothers.

A group of young people on a return visit to Barovke in the late thirties.

(*above*) A family visit from Breslev and Dvinsk to Barovke. Seated from left to right: Chaim's maternal grandmother, his father and mother; front row, first on right: Chaim next to his sister. Standing: Merke, cousin Sonja, Uncle Chaim from Breslev and Chaim's sister Sonja.

(*below*) Outside their neighbour's house; seated: Chaim's mother, Leba, Titania's daughter and Titania.

(*above*) An early visit to Barovke after the war; on the far left, Motte Panz; on the far right, Matis Frost. The woman with the headscarf and bag is Bluma Rosin, the man behind her to her right, Reuven Panz. The man with the white hat, holding the gate, is Mendel Fleishman.

(*below*) A visit to Barovke's memorial in 1968; Reuven Panz is to the left of the monument, with the white peaked cap and glasses.

Chaim's parents on holiday in the sixties in Ayre.

Chaim in the sixties.

(*above*) Chaim by the lake, (*below*) the lake and surrounding countryside of Barovke.

Chaim's return visit to Barovke in 1990.

'When I returned to Barovke in 1990 only one Jew was left…who looked like a tortoise which had been winkled out of its shell.'

'What do I think of Karlis Ulmanis? *Es shteyt in posek* ...'
'What is Hitler up to?'
'Hitler? *Di gemore zogt* ...'

And *die gemore* indeed had something to say about everything, much of it wise, but not a little of it irrelevant, and though in my younger years I admired father's ability to draw guidance from the ancient texts, I became exasperated with it as I grew older. He had a good command of language and could speak with clarity and force, but I always knew what he was going to say before he had said it. He had a well-stocked library, but with much the same books, and a well-stocked mind but with much the same material. The secular books which my sisters received as school prizes, together with a few Yiddish classics by Shalom Aleichem and Peretz, were kept on a different shelf in a different room in case they should contaminate the sacred ones.

He sometimes read a newspaper and, in later years, Churchill's *History of World War II* – which he probably read in homage to the great man – but apart from that I never saw him hold a secular work in his hands. Even when he tried to teach himself English in Glasgow, he did so, or tried to do so, via an English translation of the Old Testament and the Talmud, and he would come out with expressions like 'hast thou had a good day?'

He liked to quote the Hebrew expression, *mikol lomdai hiskalti* – I have learned from all my pupils – but there were very few people in Barovke from whom he could learn anything at all. Shimshon Ber, and the others members of his little Talmudic group, may have loved scholarship but they weren't scholars and they kept going over old ground without touching upon new insights, which is why he cherished any chance visitor who was truly learned. Every time he went to Dvinsk he made a pilgrimage to the house of the Ragachover Gaon, perhaps the greatest Jewish sage of the day, in the hope of picking up some stray aside on which he could ponder.

Most of our visitors, as I explained earlier, were *meshullochim*, charity collectors, some of whom had been to every country in Europe, and even to America. It was largely from them that father derived his knowledge of the wider Jewish world.

S'i alts hefker was their constant refrain, nothing counted for anything. People lived freer lives, and some of them lived prosperous lives. But there was no Sabbath, no festivals, no *kashrut*, and if children were given a Jewish education at all they learned just about enough Hebrew to say Kaddish – the memorial prayer – for their parents. And the further west one moved, the worse it got, as Jews by the thousand were marrying out of their faith or were otherwise lost to Judaism.

The more father heard from them the more he became reconciled to Latvia and his little domain in Barovke. It may not have widened his horizons, but it did not threaten his values, and if people were denied the sort of freedom or opportunities they enjoyed in England or America, he, for one, could live without them.

Latvia was in fact changing under his very eyes and, in 1934, Karlis Ulmanis, founder and head of the Peasants Party, who previously served as prime minister, disolved parliament and made himself dictator.

The idea of living under a dictatorship did not seem to trouble anyone in Barovke unduly, possibly because their experience of living in a free society was limited. The main question, usually discussed in hushed voices, was not whether Ulmanis was good or bad for Latvia, but whether he was good or bad for the Jews, and the consensus seemed to be that while he wasn't all that good, he could have been worse. He regarded small farmers as the backbone of the nation and naturally favoured them, which meant that everyone else, including the Jews, who were overwhelmingly townsmen, were treated with disfavour. The economy, moreover, was rigidly controlled and Jews suffered from bureaucratic obstruction.

After the coup, political parties were suppressed, the free press was abolished, and the government ruled by decree. Yet if Latvia was a dictatorship, the atmosphere was less oppressive than in Poland, which was still nominally a democracy, and our relatives over the border wished that their situation was half as fortunate as ours.

There was a huge photograph in the *pahzharne*, showing

Ulmanis, a large, white-haired, red-faced, smiling figure, receiving a garland from a small girl. There was another in the school hall, and other, smaller ones in every classroom, and, if I remember rightly, there was also one in the *atchosa*, the public lavatory, all of them in the same pose with the same little girl.

Moishe Zeitlin had Karlis Ulmanis in a gilded frame, like an icon, over his counter. We even had one somewhere in the house, and I must say, dictator or not, Ulmanis looked kindly and avuncular, like a clean-shaven Santa Claus.

The local representative of central authority was the *natshalnik*. He was guest of honour at the Latvian Independence Day service held annually in the main synagogue, and would sit by the ark, with his chain of office round his neck and a large black *yarmulke* on his head, breathing heavily and following the service in a Latvian translation.

I could not take my eyes off him for he was the fattest man I had ever seen, with several underchins and a vast corporation which sagged between his legs and which threatened to reach the floor. He would, at several points in the service, drop off to sleep and there was something mildly reassuring about his sleepiness and his size. It made authority seem less intimidating.

Father, however, dreaded the occasion. He had to say a prayer in Latvian for Karlis Ulmanis, Defence Minister Janis Balodis, and other members of his administration, all of them ending in 'is', and he got into the habit of adding an 'is' suffix to every word he uttered. He spent hours going over the text with Abrasha Pinchashovits to make sure that he got his pronunciation right, but when it came to the actual performance he was a bundle of nerves. His voice quivered, his face turned white, he sweated, as if he would be sent packing if he got a word wrong or uttered an 'is' too many, or too few.

The *natchalnik* lived in Dvinsk and we only saw him once or twice a year and the men who actually exercised authority in Barovke were Jan, the village policeman, whom I have already described, and Tolk, who was with the border police.

The former was in field grey, with grey hair, grey eyes and grey voice, and spent much of his time writing reports, scrutinizing papers and stamping permits, of which there were a great many. He was not in the least officious and if papers were not quite in order he tried to smooth things out with a higher authority. If he was at all typical of the Latvian police, then the Latvian police were wonderful.

Tolk was another matter. He was robustly built, red-faced in khaki, with a forage cap on his head, a cartridge belt round his waist, and a rifle slung across his back. Jan was rarely seen outside his house, which also served as the police station, but Tolk would patrol the district on horseback, and what with his rifle, his cartridges and horse, he exuded an air of authority and menace and I would flee at the sight of him. Then one evening as he was cantering across the cobbled square, his rifle went off, his horse reared up on its hind legs and he toppled to the ground. I did not witness the incident, but a hundred people did. There is nothing like a tumble to reduce a man to human proportions and he became less intimidating.

Latvia may have ceased to be a democracy but it was still regarded as something of a *goldener medine* – a golden land – by Jews in Poland, and there was hardly a week in which Tolk did not apprehend some poor wretch trying to smuggle himself across the border. Some, however, made it as far as Barovke where they would find refuge with one family or another until they could be passed on to a safer place.

Zussman was under particular suspicion because he lived on the edge of the forest which straddled the border. His house was raided on a number of occasions, and every time he carried a load of hay Tolk would prod it with his bayonet. Beirach was once found harbouring an illegal immigrant and was heavily fined, but everyone chipped in to pay the fine.

As Barovke was on the border smuggling was always rife. However, it became something of a cottage industry after Poland dumped vast quantities of sugar in Latvia at giveaway prices, while the price in Poland itself remained high and during the hours of darkness the forests teemed with shadowy figures humping huge sacks of sugar on their backs.

The people whom Tolk usually caught were woodsmen and

peasants but he was convinced that the big operators, the people who actually organized the traffic, were Jews and he asked father to warn his congregants from the pulpit of the dangerous game they were playing.

'Do I have to tell my flock not to break the law?' said father. 'I do it every time I open my mouth.'

At which Tolk wagged a finger at him.

'I know you Jews think you're all clever, but don't you start thinking that we're all idiots.'

'An anti-Semite,' said father, which he possibly was.

Yet his son Wovik, a bouncy, freckle-faced youngster with wavy hair and a toothy grin, was friendly with my sisters and often helped them with their homework and when I started school I looked to him as protector against the alien hordes around me.

Authority at a rather higher level was represented by the headmaster of the local school, short, slight and bald, with yellowing features like an ivory figurine. There was something sinister about the very slightness of his form, his small hard eyes, his tight lips and huge, hairless head and when he entered a classroom everyone turned to stone.

I don't know what position he held outside school but he was obviously a man of some importance in the locality for he had a place on the dais between the *natchalnik* and the district army commander on the Independence Day parade in the village square.

I was told he hated Jews. I don't know what evidence there was for it, but from the look of lofty contempt with which he regarded the entire school at morning assembly, I had the impression that he hated everyone, Jew and Gentile alike.

Barovke had a largely Christian population, although I was barely aware of their existence, partly because the Jews lived in what might be called old Barovke, whereas most non-Jews lived either in scattered farmsteads or in the new houses, some of them of stone, which were rising along both sides of the highway to Dvinsk.

For myself, I did not regard the Christian areas as hostile territory, but I regarded every house in old Barovke as an extension of my own and obviously could not think of new Barovke in the same terms. Moreover, many non-Jews kept dogs, usually large ones, and I was afraid of their bark and their bite. Finally one had to have a port of call in new Barovke, somebody to visit, and I had none.

My sisters had any number of non-Jewish friends but then they were less shy and timid than I was, and had more time to develop friendships. They did not have to study with father every evening, as I did, they didn't go to Heder, and rarely attended synagogue. They could also speak Russian and Latvian, and were thus fairly at ease in the outside world, whereas the sort of inculcation I had received and was receiving kept me apart, and made me wary of the non-Jew.

I did, however, become friendly with Simyon, a genial giant with a long red beard and golden curls like a Greek god, who worked in the nearby timber-yard. He did any number of odd jobs in Jewish homes around Barovke, especially ours, for father was incapable of even knocking a nail into the wall, and every time a shelf collapsed, a chair got broken or a lamp ceased to light, Simyon was there to repair it.

He once killed a man in a drunken brawl, which didn't seem to trouble anyone. Jews had their shortcomings, and Gentiles had theirs, especially after they'd had a drink or two.

Simyon made me a clapper for Purim and other wooden toys, which were the only toys I had. I was rather proud of our friendship and would show him off to visiting relatives. 'He's killed a man, you know,' and Simyon, who knew more than a bit of Yiddish, was always ready to supply the details.

Jan, the policeman, had a pretty young daughter Nunka who was the best friend of my younger sister Leba. They were both blonde, both grey-eyed, and, on festive occasions, both wore the same sailor outfits, so that they sometimes looked like twins. Nunka only had sisters and adopted me as a sort of older brother. She would offer me her dolls to play with and would sometimes follow me everywhere, which I found embarrassing, and I regarded her as a nuisance rather than a friend.

My older sisters had a friend, Marintsa, a shrill, effervescent, bright-eyed, apple-cheeked girl who was in and out of our house, and father – to mother's stern disapproval – could never resist pinching her cheeks, though as far as I know he never pinched her bottom. She must have been about 12 when I was seven or eight and looked almost a woman in my eyes. I couldn't help noticing how lively and uninhibited she was compared to the Jewish girls in Barovke, who tended to be prim and restrained and who would rarely be seen away from their mothers, and she brightened a room when she entered it.

Her father was a herdsman at a nearby farm where she sometimes helped out with the cows. I was once chased by a bull and, as I could not tell a bull from a cow, I gave everything with horns a wide berth. I once asked her if she was not afraid.

'Afraid? What's there to be afraid of?' and the next evening, with a hurricane lamp in hand she took me to the cowshed.

It was bitterly cold outside, but warm and snug in the cowshed. The cows were all steaming, and a delicate mist seemed to arise from Marintsa herself.

I was nevertheless terrified, but she led me up to each of the cows in turn to show me how gentle they were, and finally she sat me down beside her and showed me how to milk them.

I was still a bit nervous for, gentle or not, they were still large, but she calmed me down, told me to dig my head into the flank and guided my hands to the teats. The milk, bubbly and warm, began to squirt into the bucket and after a minute I relaxed sufficiently to enjoy it.

The smell of the straw, the dung, the cows, the milk and of Marintza herself, was intoxicating, and in a strange way it was almost a mystical experience. Here I was in the heart of *goydom* and revelling in every minute of it!

I would hurry back to her cowshed at every opportunity. She had enlarged my universe.

Chapter 9

Saints and Sinners

The idea that children should be seen but not heard was never accepted among Jews, certainly not in Barovke. We were not only heard, we were required to perform as soon as we could speak, and in some instances even before, if only to show how far the hopes which our parents had vested in us were about to be fulfilled.

We were thus all armed with poems or songs and one could hardly attend a social gathering without one infant or another being encouraged – or sometimes forcibly propelled – to do his or her bit, usually in German, sometimes in Russian or Latvian, occasionally in Yiddish.

These gatherings were generally held on Sunday afternoons and were composed of young mothers and young children, accompanied by the occasional grandmother.

The favourite venue was Soreleh Trupin's because she had the largest drawing room but every mother took turns to act as hostess, and display her best china, her best cakes, rolls and *varenye* (homemade jam) and, above all, to display her children

I presume that Yiddish was not particularly favoured on such occasions because everyone spoke it, whereas a performance in a foreign language suggested a superior level of attainment and I remember one toothless little girl with long pigttails in a red, velvet frock who recited a poem in French. She couldn't have understood a word she said and neither did anyone else.

My own extensive repertoire – I can only remember the opening lines – included one piece in German:

In vald vil ikh lebn, in heysen zumer tsayt ... (In the forest I yearn to live in the hot summer time.)

Another in Russian:

Zautra, zaudra, ne sevodnia, kak lentiai govoriat ...(Tomorrow, tomorrow, not today, that's what all the sluggards say.)

A third in Latvian:

Ga ga ga zuseti, vei tu gribi maiseti?... (Ga ga ga my geese, are you all ready to eat?)

To which, as befits the son of a rabbi, I could have added any number of pieces in Hebrew, but these I reserved for the men-only occasions to which I accompanied father.

My German, Russian and Latvian repertoire – as my examples may suggest – was entirely secular, my Hebrew repertoire was entirely sacred. I learned to read at an early age, but even before I could read I knew whole chunks from the *siddur* (prayerbook) off by heart, and I can still recall my bedtime prayers:

'Blesed art thou, O Lord our God, King of the universe who makest the bands of sleep fall upon mine eyes and slumber upon mine eyelids. May it be thy will, O Lord, my God and God of my fathers, to let me lie down in peace and rise again in peace ...

'In the name of the Lord, the God of Israel, may Michael be at my right hand; Gabriel at my left; Uriel before me; Raphael behind me, and the divine presence above me.'

I was afraid of the dark so that I would say it all by candlelight and I could almost see the four archangels dancing around me among the flickering shadows on the wall.

There was something comforting about their very names, possibly because they sounded so much like that of my father, Azriel, and in my younger years I did tend to think of father as an earthbound member of the heavenly host, and presumed that the archangels must have looked like him. I did, however, have some trouble with 'the divine presence', and I was a little afraid of it, if only because I found it impossible to imagine, but then I was afraid of many things, some of them seen, most of them unseen.

My bedtime prayers were my first party piece, to which, as I grew older, I added whole Psalms, as well as chunks from the Mishna (the oral law), mainly for the benefit of visiting rabbis, who would pat my head, pinch my cheeks, and give me a small – a very small – coin, by way of reward.

I relished these occasions because I relished every opportunity to show off, but I was also aware that I was not only being tested on my ability as a pupil, but on father's diligence as a teacher.

Teaching his son is about the most important duty a Jewish father can have, especially if he happens to be a rabbi, and father took my education very seriously, not only out of religious obligation but, I suspect, because he regarded himself as a failure and hoped to fulfil himself through me. We thus began learning together when I was three. By the time I was four I could read Hebrew fairly fluently, without, however, being able to understand it. By the time I was five I could translate whole pages of Scripture.

Father only took the older boys into the Heder – girls didn't enter into it – aged ten or upwards, when they were of an age to be introduced to the mysteries of the Talmud, and it was something of a privilege to be in his class.

The younger boys met in the *shtibl*, the smaller, rundown synagogue, which seemed to be sinking into the ground. It had a low roof and a cast-iron stove round which we all huddled in the winter, and were taught, after a fashion, by Moshe Yudeh. We would attend classes for about three hours on Sunday mornings, and an hour and a half on weekday evenings, but beyond that father used to teach me privately every evening for an hour after supper and, in the winter, at least, that hour was perhaps my favourite time of day.

Father would rise at dawn to be in synagogue for prayers and, after a hurried breakfast would go on to the slaughter house. He slept in the afternoon, and in the early evening he would be in Heder so that, except for the Sabbath and festivals, I didn't see all that much of him, and I cherished the hour after supper when I had him all to myself.

During my evening lessons, father smoked long, four-inch Diplomat cigarettes, with tobacco only in the final inch. His beard would turn white with ash, but somehow never caught fire. We studied by the light of a kerosene lamp, and the smell of the tobacco with the smell of the kerosene somehow provided the ideal ambience for study, possibly because the lamp sent up flickering shadows which made me feel that I had Uriel, Gabriel, Raphael and Michael dancing around me. On summer evenings, however, the lessons lost much of their magic.

The cycle of the 52 portions of the Pentateuch – the *sedrah* – begins with the first chapters of Genenis at the end of October, and ends with the last in Deuteronomy twelve months later. Genesis and the first half of Exodus were a joy. They were known in Yiddish as *di vinterdike sedres* – the winter portions – and were full of colourful characters and dramatic events, the six days of creation, Adam and Eve, the expulsion from Eden, Cain and Abel, Noah's ark, the Flood, the Tower of Babel, Abraham and Sarah, the destruction of Sodom and Gomorrah, Lot and Lot's wife, the binding of Isaac, Jacob and Esau, Laban, Joseph and his brethren, the enslavement of the Israelites, the birth of Moses, the Ten Plagues, the crossing of the Red Sea, the wandering in the wilderness, the Ten Commandments ...

When I sat with father in his small book-lined room, with blizzards raging outside, those tales of distant times in distant lands were more than enough to compensate for the rigours of winter. I couldn't wait for the lessons to begin and was always sorry when they finished.

By the spring, however, when the Israelites were stalled in the wilderness, the pace of events slowed down. There were still moments of drama, like the story of the golden calf, the rebellion of Korah, and Balaam and his talking ass, but there were also endless begettings and inventories and arcane passages.

'If a woman be delivered of a man child, then she shall be unclean seven days, as in the days of her impurity of her sickness she shall be unclean ... But if she bear a maid-child she shall be unclean two weeks, as in her impurity; and she shall continue in the blood of purification ... '

I became restless and fidgety, especially when the broad beams of the setting sun began pouring in through the open windows and I could hear the shrill sounds of friends at play. I was normally proud to be my father's son, but at such times I regarded it as a misfortune.

I didn't actually object to the lessons, I was too docile for that, but evaded the text by asking awkward questions, and the older I got the more awkward they became.

Why was the mother unclean for only a week if the child was a boy, and two weeks if she was a girl? Why did she become unclean at all? What was the blood of purification? Who did it purify? And if the blood purified, why was she unclean?

Father's standard reply was, 'You'll understand when you're older,' though I'm not sure if I understand even now.

Heder lessons tended to be tedious summer or winter, but they at least offered the prospect of company, for I liked to be in a crowd even where I was not fully part of it. There was also the hope of diversions for Moishe Yudeh, though the kindest and mildest of men could, if sufficiently provoked – and we made it our business to provoke him sufficiently – became a raging fury.

I often went over the same ground with Moishe Yudeh that I had trodden with father but I didn't mind, for I could at least display my superior knowledge. However, we also studied the Shulchan Oruch, the code of Jewish law, and there I was in trouble.

The Hebrew script of the Pentateuch was vowelled, which the Shulchan Oruch was not, and I stumbled over every word. As if to encourage me to greater effort, Moishe Yudeh would thump me on the back every time I stumbled and would sometimes thump me even if I didn't stumble.

And thumping was the least of it. There would always be a miscreant who would make a rude noise, discharge a stink bomb or set free a frog or white mouse. Yudeh might ignore one incident and the attendant sniggers, and even a second, but if they continued without a break – as they often did – his ashen features turned a dark red, the veins on his brow stood out like creepers, and we dived for cover before he exploded. But he always managed to grab hold of someone – usually my friend Welfke – twist his ear till it almost came away in his hand, or whack him repeatedly about the head. I don't think he ever broke bones or drew blood, but must have come fairly near it, and we all had marks to show for his tutelage.

Our parents loved us dearly, but they never questioned the divine right of a master to mutilate his pupils, and we accepted our punishment as no more than our due. Moreover, as we could see from the very texts before us, he treated us no worse than the God of Israel treated the children of Israel. Suffering was part of our creed.

In any case his thump and his whacks were not half as painful as his lessons, for he spoke in a low monotone, half muffled by his moustache and could make even the story of Joseph in Egypt sound tedious.

He was a different man outside Heder, not genial certainly, but kindly, helpful, solicitous. His trouble was that he hated small boys.

Unusually for a man in a semi-ecclesiastical occupation, he had a hobby, wood-carving. He didn't carve figurines, for that would have been against Jewish law – 'thou shalt not make unto thyself a graven image' – but he did carve paper knives as sharp as daggers and as lethal, though as far as I remember he never used them in class.

When I was six I enrolled in the village school. Everyone in and around Barovke could make themselves understood in two or three languages, and a smattering of Latvian was one of them but until I started school I rarely heard it used in the normal course of conversation, except when we went to the post office and would not be served unless we could explain our needs in Latvian. At school itself, however, one heard nothing but Latvian, and if one used Russian or Yiddish in the playground one had to take care not to be overheard by the teachers.

My sisters, who were fairly proficient in the language, gave me a number of lessons and warned me that I must learn to call Barovke, Silene, and Dvinsk, Daugavpils.

'What do you call Barovke?'

'Silene.'

'And Dvinsk?'

'Daugavpils.'

That much I remembered, but forgot everything else and found myself being instructed in a foreign language, which was true of nearly everyone else in the class, and we sat around in a daze.

School involved other novelties. We had to sit in class bare-headed, and as I had previously only uncovered my head when I went for a haircut or a swim, I felt half naked. The sensation added to my natural awkwardness, and at first I could not do anything right.

I knew about a dozen Gentiles and was on fairly friendly terms with some of them, but a roomful of non-Jews, albeit young ones, was a fairly intimidating experience. They seemed sturdier, bigger and rougher than the Jewish boys I knew. At first I was nervous of them, especially during playtime, and braced myself for some sort of private pogrom, but they were indifferent to me and I soon got used to them. In any case I could, if need be, always look to my sister's friend Wovik – who was four or five years older than me – for protection. I had to go to Poland before I suffered my first private pogrom, and that was at a Jewish school.

Our teacher Alechne, was a tall, lean figure, ramrod straight, with broad shoulders, a military stride, and short cropped hair like a Prussian Junker. He was an officer in the reserves and could be seen in full uniform on horseback, at the Independence Day parade.

He spent much of the first day striding round the room and berating us at the top of his voice, as a drill sergeant might berate new recruits and even if we didn't understand what he was saying we knew damned well what he meant.

As an introduction to the new Latvia it was an alarming experience. As I've said, I also dreaded the headmaster, who would glide noiselessly along the corridors and my blood chilled when he suddenly appeared out of nowhere like a genie from a bottle. He was known round the school as the poison-dwarf, but exuded an authority out of all proportion to his size, or, indeed, his sound.

I can't say I ever grew to love the place, for in any case schools are not there to be loved, but there were things about it which filled me with awe.

First of all there was Alechne himself. With the possible exception of Abrasha Pinchashavits, I had never been in close proximity to such a magnificent figure, and Pinchashavits, tall and handsome though he was, had wavy hair and a neat moustache, which softened his appearance, while Alechne looked as if he might have been hewn out of granite. He was like a god in my eyes, not the God of Israel, whom I imagined as long-haired, bearded and in flowing robes, but a Gentile god, a Nordic god. A Thor. My older sisters were both in love with him. I am not sure if I wasn't, and Shaike, who was in my class obviously modelled himself on him, and tried to adopt his strut.

Secondly, there was the school building, which had only recently been completed. I had never been in such clean and spacious surroundings. Jewish homes, synagogues, classrooms were all poorly maintained, cramped, overcrowded, overheated, badly lit and poorly ventilated. The school rooms were large and lofty with tall windows letting in broad shafts of light, and even the surrounding fields, instead of being overgrown, were so neatly cropped that they looked like carpets. And all the teachers, men and women, were well spoken and neatly dressed, the men neatly shaved, the women perfumed and neatly coiffured.

In Heder one had old Moishe Yudeh with his straggly beard, plaintive voice and shabby clothes, thumping one boy, pulling the ear of another, and barely audible above the chaos. In school one hesitated to breathe without permission. It was my first experience of order and, certainly at the beginning, I rather liked it.

I thanked God in my morning prayers for not making me a Gentile (or a woman), but it seemed to me that the Gentiles had rather a lot going for them.

And finally there were the books. In Heder and, indeed, at home, they were all – apart from a few books won by my sisters as school prizes – in black with cloth covers and yellowing pages, crumbling at the edges, which sometimes came away in one's hand, and the nearest thing to an illustration in any of them was about a dozen lines showing how the Israelites were encamped round the Sanctuary in the wilderness.

On my first day at school, however, I was presented with a

brand new book with white covers, large, clear letters and so fresh
and clean that one could smell the print on the pages and the glue
in the binding. It also had dozens of pictures, some of them in
colour, of kings and queens, of castles and palaces, of battles with
men on horseback brandishing swords and axes. It was all in
Latvian, of course, and months passed before I could understand
a word of it, but it became my greatest treasure and I could not
tear myself away from it.

I also began leafing through my sisters' school books with equal
fascination, for they had pictures of different cities which were only
names to me, Vienna, Berlin, Paris. Father could not have failed to
notice the zeal with which I approached my school texts, and the
reluctance with which I sometimes approached the sacred ones.

I was about eight when I began to suspect that I was something
of a disappointment to father. There is a general belief among Jews
and Scotsmen that sons of the manse are, or should be, preternaturally bright, and while I was not preternaturally stupid it soon
became clear that I did not have the makings of another Leipkaleh.
Father in fact taught us together for a while, possibly in the hope
that something of Leipkaleh's genius might rub off on to me, but it
began to look as if something of my lethargy might rub off on to
Leipkaleh and, much to my relief, father abandoned the effort.

Although my earliest ambition was to be a rabbi, which indeed,
was the ambition he had for me, rabbis, it was believed, were born
and not made and he soon came to feel that I not only lacked the
aptitude but the application. I was keen enough, he said, when it
came to *mayselekh* – little stories – but seemed indifferent to
everything else. Moishe Yudeh had advised him that I was a less
than zealous student, which came as less than a surprise. I
performed my religious duties religiously, but without
enthusiasm. I said my bedtime prayers carefully, but garbled my
morning prayers, and during school term, when I had to be out of
the house first thing in the morning, I sometimes combined them
with my breakfast or left them half said, for I would much rather
have faced up to the wrath of God than the wrath of Alechne.

Father used to tell me how he grew up with two boys who went
on to Slobodka Yeshiva and became *tsadikim*, saints, but they had

a glow about them even as children, as if the divine presence was already hovering over them. I evidently lacked that glow and if I lacked it as a child I was unlikely to acquire it as an adult. From what I could see, his precious Leipkaleh was equally glowless, but he had other things going for him. I didn't.

My two older sisters were doing well at school, and the eldest one was doing brilliantly, but that was no consolation: they were girls.

He would comfort himself with the thought that I was in the last resort a *voyler yingl*, a good boy, but he was soon to discover that I wasn't even that.

At about this time, when I was eight, it so happened that there was a vacancy for a *shochet* in Glasgow and my uncle, who was chairman of the board of Shechita (he was chairman of the board of almost everything else), offered father the job. From then events followed in rapid succession. It was decided father would go to Glasgow (borrowing the necessary fare from uncle) and would send for us as soon as he had saved enough for the tickets, which might take a year. In the meantime, my eldest sister, who had finished elementary school in Barovke, would go to a gymnasium in Dvinsk, I would be sent to Breslev and my other sisters would remain in Barovke with my mother.

I left for Breslev some time before father left for Glasgow and he accompanied me on foot as far as the Polish border (there was room beside me on the open cart but he wanted to save the fare). It was a blazing hot day and he kept removing his homburg and wiping his hatband and forehead. The horse was plodding slowly along the dry, rutted track and I kept dropping off to sleep. Father and I never had much to say to one another, especially when we had much to say and were, I think, rendered inarticulate by affection. When we reached the border father blessed me, but we did not kiss or cry, for we have always been afraid, or reluctant, or perhaps unable, to show emotion in our family, and to that extent we were Englishmen ready made.

I continued onwards towards Breslev while father returned towards Barovke, and I watched his erect black-clad figure recede through the haze of a hot afternoon. He did not turn round once.

Chapter 10

Return to Breslev

Where Barovke was a *shtetaleh*, Breslev was a *shtetl* with a population of about 5,000, including some 3,000 Jews.

There were proper roads and pavements in Breslev and there was even a small railway station on the edge of town. It had no electricity, mains sewage or running water, but they were on the way. A new housing estate on the outskirts known as the Domques already had all three, but it was reserved for new Polish settlers, representatives of the New Poland. Jews, Russians and Ukrainians were firmly excluded.

Barovke virtually had no history. Breslev could trace its origins back to the sixteenth century and even beyond and was initially part of greater Lithuania. In the seventeenth century it came under Polish rule, in the eighteenth century under Russian rule and was recovered by Poland in 1921 in the course of the Russo-Polish war. It was occupied by Russia in 1939, invaded by Germany in 1941, liberated by Russia in 1944 and is now in the independent republic of Belorussia.

Breslev, like Barovke, was surrounded by lakes and forests but while Barovke and its surroundings were flat, Breslev had what is called a *barg*, a mountain, or, to give it its full name *der schloss barg*, the castle mountain, for it was crowned by the ruins of a fortress.

The mountain could not have been more than about 600 feet above sea level and took a few minutes to ascend, which I frequently did and, on my first ascent on a clear morning in early autumn, I looked round and beheld what, to my eyes, was a metropolis.

In the distance, on one side, was the railway station. On the other, one could see the red roofs and white walls of the Domques. At the foot was the main street, Pilsudskiya Ulitze, flanked at one end by stone buildings three or even four storeys high. Beyond them were the lakes, one large (the Drywiata) and one small (the Nowiata), with wooden craft bobbing on the water. The two were linked by a narrow neck of water which was crossed by a bridge.

In the summer the lakes were some distance from Breslev. When the snows began to melt in the spring they grew until they lapped on the very edges of the town and there were folk memories of a flood which had completely destroyed it.

The buildings were nondescript, and the only ones which linger in the memory are an old windmill with large wooden sails, and the blue and white Greek Orthodox church with its domes bunched together like a cluster of onions.

Breslev had numerous synagogues, including a cluster of three or four *minyanim* (houses of prayer) built round a large cobbled courtyard which also housed the fire brigade with its huge, brightly painted wooden barrels and gleaming hand pumps. The brigade, as in Barovke, was manned by volunteers.

There was also a *yeshiva*, two Jewish day schools, a Jewish bank, a hospital, even a theatre. There was no public transport but the sight of cars, vans and lorries was not uncommon and there was the constant clatter of horsedrawn vehicles on the cobbled streets, while the streets themselves were flanked by wooden pavements (*trotuars*).

Most of the homes, as in Barovke, were of timber with sagging windows and steep roofs, but while every house in Barovke stood among trees in its own plot of land, Pilsudskiya Ulitza, which ran from one end of the town to the other, was barren and treeless and any gardens and courtyards were tucked away at the back. The whole place seemed slightly dejected, but that was possibly because I felt more than slightly dejected myself.

In Barovke I was crown prince. In Breslev, though mother's family enjoyed some prominence, I was nobody, unknown and largely unseen. I was nine months in the town and did not make a single friend and those months were among the most desolate of my life.

I normally have a retentive memory, at least for distant events, but when it comes to Breslev I can recall few faces – apart, of course, from those of my family – and only three or four names.

One was Gilliskovsky, one of my father's friends. I remember him not because I had anything to do with him or had exchanged as much as a word with him, but because he was such a magnificent figure, a dandy in a white suit, white boater, with small pointed beard and flowing moustache, twirling a bamboo cane, like an Edwardian boulevardier. I also remember him because he was always smiling, and smiles were rare in Breslev.

Another was Shneir Aron. Men of substance in Latvia and Poland tended to be substantial men, and he was a large, portly figure with a neat little beard and large glasses. He owned the fishing rights to several lakes in the neighbourhood and his name frequently cropped up in conversation because he was a generous benefactor of the school I attended, the local hospital and numerous other institutions. He and his wife were on friendly terms with my grandmother and when he took me there on a visit we were served tea by a silent but elegantly dressed young woman in black with a white lace cap whom I took to be their daughter, though in the course of the afternoon it gradually dawned upon me that she may have been their servant. They lived in a house as large as Barovke school with lofty ceilings and paintings on the wall. There was a bowl on the table filled with fruit I had never seen, and certainly never tasted before, oranges, bananas and grapes. I was given a grape. It was so delicious that when no one was looking I helped myself to two or three more, and spent a sleepless night in case Shneir Aron should have counted his grapes and charged me with theft.

A third was another of my father's friends, Chaim Isaac. He lived in a small house with a large wife and innumerable children, and he told me that he had been to England and come back, to which his wife added in a weary voice, 'He's been everywhere and come back.'

He seemed too old to have small children, but he was bottle-feeding an infant on his lap as he spoke to me, while another was crawling at his feet, and I could barely hear him above the shrieks and screams which filled the air.

He described England as a *golderneh medineh mit golderneh mentshen*, a golden land with golden people, but he didn't much care for London. 'It had no beginning and no end,' he said, and one could walk through it for a week without getting away from it. It was also a difficult place to find a livelihood.

'Especially if you're useless and lazy,' added his wife.

It was Chaim Isaac who gave me my first taste of *halva*, which is possibly why I remember him at all. Had I not been a glutton my failure of memory might have been complete.

I remember the rabbi of Breslev – though I have forgotten his name. He was tall and thin with a face so white it almost glowed, and a tall fur hat, so that he had to stoop when he entered a room. He had a plaintive, high-pitched voice which rose to a shriek in moments of excitement, and a long white beard – the longest beard I have ever seen – like brushed flax which extended beyond his navel. He was spoken of as a saint. His grandson, a thick-set little thug, was my principal tormentor.

Everyone else, teachers, schoolmates, neighbours, I have forgotten. There are some events so painful that they etch themselves on the memory and cannot be forgotten. Others less painful, but still unhappy, obliterate themselves of their own accord.

I have even forgotten the season, but then by the time I came to Breslev the summer – which was the season I lived for – was behind me and I left in the spring. Even winter can have its joys and there must have been skiing on the hill, skating on the frozen lakes, snowmen and snow fights, but I couldn't have had any part in them for I remember nothing of them.

Nor can I recall anything of the prolonged cycle of Tishrei festivals, neither Rosh Hashonoh nor Yom Kippur, nor Succoth, and the only thing I do remember was that one of my uncles got drunk on Simchas Torah and kept calling for his dead father. Such total obliteration suggests total distress.

My mother's family, as I was often told, had been ruined in the Russian Revolution, and my understanding of ruin was poverty, but they had a large two-storey house with spacious rooms and a living-in servant, outhouses and a huge courtyard. In Barovke we formed separate compartments in the house by moving around wardrobes; in Breslev the rooms were separated by actual walls, and they lived better with their poverty than we with our prosperity.

The family's flax and corn business with a flour mill was managed by my uncle Yankel, and a warehouse which was looked after by another uncle Chaim Kasre. Rachmiel, the youngest brother, who was short with elaborately coiffured hair, studied architecture. He married during the course of my stay without as yet being in regular employment – so that the business supported four families and helped out a fifth. Aaron Mattis, the oldest son, had left Poland some years previously to study painting in Paris which, in those days, had a fairly large colony of Jewish artists from eastern Europe.

Aaron was gifted, but not so gifted as to earn a living from his work, or even pay for his expenses. He moved to Palestine where he met and married a young American medical student and they settled in Chicago, where he found it difficult to earn a livelihood. Their two daughters, Rochelle and Elinor, are my only surviving cousins.

My own parents were a source of considerable expenditure to the family during their unhappy years in Breslev and I suspect they may have been helped out with the occasional *zloty* even after they moved to Barovke.

Grandmother worked in the warehouse, I never discovered in what capacity, but it kept her busy for most part of the day, which didn't mean that she neglected me completely. She made sure that I said my prayers first thing in the morning and last thing at night, that I changed my underwear regularly and that I left for school with a scrubbed face and neatly attired. She also inspected my hands regularly to make sure that my nails were clean and that I didn't bite them, but never unbent sufficiently to pat my head, pinch my cheek, or utter a word of affection. She had brought up six children amidst great difficulties and took no great pleasure in being burdened with another at her age in life. She obviously regarded me as a nuisance, and a nuisance I soon became.

Uncle Yankel looked a kindly man, with a cigarette always smouldering on his lips, and three days' stubble on his chin in what might now be called an Arafat beard. He had a beaming expression and genial manner, and one could always tell his approach by his loud smoker's cough, but he lived some distance away and I saw little of him.

Chaim Kasre, who had married some five years previously, lived with grandmother. He had a tall, handsome wife, sallow-skinned, dark eyed, dark haired, with dimpled cheeks and a magnificent bosom. They occupied a large room on the first floor with frosted glass doors and I would sometimes watch her in silhouette as she dressed or undressed, until Polyna, the maid, caught me and boxed my ears.

They had a three-year-old daughter, a tiny exquisite thing with huge blue eyes and a cascade of golden curls who had a habit of following me round the house and wouldn't go to sleep until I kissed her good night.

Chaim Kasre was tall, well built with blue eyes and short, cropped blond hair. He looked German to me and had Germanic ways. Though he was the younger brother I had the feeling that he was in charge of the whole operation and that if any serious problems arose he had to sort them out. He had also inherited grandfather's mantle as a member of the local Jewish community council, and had the stooping posture and grave air of a man with many problems on his shoulders. On the other hand he liked a vodka and after a drink or two something like a sheepish grin spread over his face and he became positively amiable. He would pat my head or give me a playful kick on my backside, but otherwise he and his wife were indifferent to my existence, except when I intruded upon theirs, which I sometimes did.

My mother had a younger sister called Leika. Tall, slender, stately, with red hair and green eyes, she was spoken of as a great beauty, but she was stricken with Bell's palsy and though she still carried herself like a queen, she looked thin, haggard and red-eyed and when she tried to smile, it looked like a grimace.

She was a qualified teacher, but when she married, grandma bought her a shop selling various textile goods, which was managed by her husband Welfke.

Welfke was a picture of a man, tall, with broad shoulders, wavy hair and a neat moustache. As it was difficult to prosper in Poland, the business was not particularly successful and Welfke took out his frustrations on Leika and sometimes beat her. The palsy, of course, added to her torments and Welfke told her to her face that he could not bear to look at her and what had begun as a great romance had turned into a martyrdom.

They had a boy of four with long, blond hair, and a dark-haired girl of three both shrill and lively, who also had the habit of following me around.

Their house was full of toys and, young though they were, I sometimes played with them because I'd never had any toys myself and I could get a certain amount of pleasure even out of a set of building blocks, though their main pleasure lay in throwing the blocks at me.

Welfke's features would soften at their sight, and he would get down on all fours to play with them. At such times he looked human, even lovable. At others, he could be the complete thug and the one time I actually witnessed a brawl in a synagogue he was at the centre of the affray and came home with a black eye and a bleeding nose.

The nearest thing I had to friend or companion in Breslev was Polyna. Small, slight and white-haired, she had been with grandma for years and was almost her age.

We found it difficult to communicate because she spoke Polish which I was slow to pick up, but she knew some Yiddish so we somehow managed. She darned my socks, ironed my shirts, and taught me, finally, how to tie my boot-laces. She was also the cook, at least on weekdays, and a fairly good one, but like grandma she could be fairly severe, and would often upbraid me for my untidiness.

'I've never known anything like it,' she kept complaining.
'When others eat they may leave a messy plate, or a messy table,
you mess up the whole house.'

She saw to it that I washed before meals, and said grace
afterwards – and not the truncated version, but the full one and
complained that while I rushed through my prayers I was slow at
everything else.

She watched me with impatience once as I tried to cut my
fingernails and sent clippings flying all over the room. She grabbed
the scissors and finished the job for me, after which she pared my
nails on a weekly basis, squeezing my hands warmly as she did so.
She never gave me any other sign of affection, but her face always
lit up when I came home in the evening and I had the feeling she
liked to have me around, which was not the case with anyone else
in the house. I doubt if I would have survived without her.

I was unhappy from the day I arrived until the day I left. The
most immediate cause of my distress was that I was separated
from my family, not so much my mother and sisters, who were
just over the border, but my father who, as I saw it, was at the
other end of the globe. Not that border crossings were a simple
matter in those days, but I found some reassurance in the idea of
propinquity.

Grandma being – by Breslev standards – a woman of means
was importuned by a constant succession of *meshullochim*, all of
them bearded, all of them in black, and some of whom looked like
father. I was not, even as a child, easily drawn to tears, but when
a *meshullach*, with a dark red beard, who was waiting to see
grandma, pulled out a Diplomat cigarette, lit it and blew out a
cloud of smoke, I broke down, for even if I couldn't see father that
moment, I could smell him.

The poor *meshullach* stood up in bewilderment.

'*Vos hob ikh geton?*' he asked. What have I done? I fled from the
room without answering.

Father represented kindness, warmth, tenderness and, as I was
then still religious, the divine presence. Not that mother was cold
– at least to me – but one felt that any warmth she displayed was
dutiful, whereas in father it was natural. He radiated kindliness.

I missed my daily lessons with him and would gladly have gone through the endless and meaningless passages about the sacrificial cult in Leviticus which used to darken my spring evenings, if only he had been around to explain them.

Of course, I missed mother too and my sisters, especially Lupke, who, at six, had become something of a companion.

I missed Barovke itself and even if I was denied the place I thought I deserved in the gang hierarchy, I felt that I was essentially among friends. In Breslev I felt I was among enemies. I had been warned about the anti-Semitism I would encounter among non-Jews. No one prepared me for the anti-Chaimism I would encounter among the Jews – especially at school which I loathed from the day I arrived and which I continued to loathe till the day I left.

It was called Yavneh, and was richly recommended to my parents as the best Jewish school in Breslev.

In religious terms it was middle-of-the-road, traditional rather than strictly orthodox. Some of the lessons were in Yiddish, some in Hebrew, some in Polish (which was Greek to me). I can't recall what, if anything I learned, and the only thing I do recall was the bullying. And perhaps worse than the bullying, which is something every small boy has to live through, was the isolation, which in turn was perhaps the cause of the bullying.

When one arrives at a new school at the age of five or six and enters one's first year, one is a stranger among strangers. If one arrives at the age of eight, especially from a foreign country, one is a stranger among established cliques, with their own games and their own rules and their own passwords.

When I later arrived in Glasgow at the age of nine, it should have been worse, for I was among Gentiles, and I didn't speak the same language, but I was immediately taken under the wing of a teacher – Agnes B. Smith, bless her – who made sure that I was accepted and integrated, and appointed the class captain as my superintendent and guide.

In Breslev I was left to my own devices, and having no devices I was left on my own, wandering haplessly between this crowd and that, but excluded by them all, so that the bullying which accompanied the isolation was perhaps the less painful part of the experience.

I was a foreigner, a Latvian, which was bad enough, though I should imagine that with my sunken chest, sunken cheeks and dejected appearance, I possibly invited persecution. And then came the worst incident of all, and which still rankles with me some 60 years after it happened.

The pride of the school was the new gymnasium which had a highly polished floor. It was also used for assemblies and one morning as we were waiting for assembly to begin a number of boys began skidding across it, leaving deep marks on the floor. I was far too timid – or well behaved – to join the fun, but a teacher appeared, looked at the floor, and demanded to know who was responsible, and the culprits, as one, all pointed to me.

Before I could even open my mouth I was pulled by the ear past chortling lines of youngsters to the headmaster.

'You're the new boy, aren't you? And a rabbi's son. Aren't you ashamed of yourself?

I tried to protest my innocence but he waved my words away, ordered me to stay in after school and polish the floor.

That afternoon as I got down on all fours I began to wonder if there really was a God. For all my religiosity I had never expected miracles from heaven, but I did expect elementary justice.

After school I would run home for a bite and would then go on for a further two hours of study at Heder, where my *bête noire* was the aforementioned rabbi's grandson who for no reason that I could understand would follow me on the way home and set upon me like a wild dog.

There was a *yeshiva* in Breslev, not a proper one like in Slobodka, but a *yeshiva ketano* – a small *yeshiva* – with some 60 boys aged from about nine to 15 years. It was an impoverished establishment and could not afford to feed its students and different boys would eat on different days with different families, and one boy called Reuven ate with us on Wednesdays.

He was slightly older than me and slightly taller, but he was as thin and sallow as I was, and Polyna thought we looked like brothers. He came from a small village and was as unhappy in Breslev as I was.

'But we're leaving,' he said, 'everybody is. We're going to the Argentine. We've got all the papers, all we're waiting for is money from an uncle.'

I became friendly with him and he taught me to play draughts. Studies at *yeshiva* began at dawn and continued till night so that I did not see much of him, but his Wednesday visits became the highlight of my week. Then one day he waltzed in with beaming features to announce that the money from his uncle had finally arrived and that they would be leaving in a week. He promised to write to me, but I saw no more of him and heard nothing from him.

He was replaced by a plump, pink-faced youngster, in a black hat, with a high-pitched voice, who looked as if he had eaten some good meals in his time. At his first meal at grandma's, he tested me on the extent of my Jewish knowledge and, not being satisfied with the result, he continued with his meal in silence, after which he ignored me.

He was eventually replaced by a much older boy, almost a man, with a few wisps of hair on his chin by way of a beard and dangling side-curls. He wore a large black hat like my father, but with a short crown, and a long, black, threadbare coat. He was tall and thin with blue, watery eyes behind large glasses, and a reddish patch between his nose and chin, as if he had a permanent cold, which he possibly did. He was very polite, greeted everyone with a slight bow and a timid smile, and but for his 'thank yous' every time a dish was served or removed, he never uttered a word. He always carried a sacred tome which he consulted between courses, swaying back and forth as he did so. Polyna treated him with great deference. His name was Nosson and he had such an air of sanctity about him that I felt uncomfortable in his presence and could not eat properly until he had left the table. And yet I was glad to have him around, not because he was company of sorts but because I liked to think that something of his sanctity rubbed off on to me, and there came a point where I used him as a sort of father confessor.

Being left on my own for hours on end, I explored Breslev in all directions and one evening came upon the new suburb of the Domques.

A large chunk of Belorussia, including Breslev, had been seized by the Poles in 1921 in the Russo-Polish war and Poland brought new settlers into the area, and built new estates, like the Domques, to accommodate them.

The Domques had wide tree-lined streets, and the homes, though not large, were neat with red roofs and white walls with small gardens, and to my eyes it represented the last word in luxury and elegance.

They were adding to it all the time and I would return to the place again and again to watch the concrete mixers and other machinery, all of which were new to me. I usually came at dusk, so that I could see the streetlights go on. There were youngsters at play who usually regarded me with indifference, but one evening I was set upon by a group of boys who knocked me to the ground, and I came away bleeding and bruised. This was my first experience of what might be called applied anti-Semitism.

A few weeks later I was wandering down the main street, and passed a red-haired, one-legged youngster who was sitting on an upturned barrel with a crutch by his side.

I may have paused to stare because, although there were any number of amputees around, I had never seen anyone so young with one leg before and when I turned I noticed he was following me. I quickened my pace, he quickened his. I began to run, but he was quicker on his one leg than I was with my two. He was soon abreast and gave me a whack in the face with his crutch which knocked two of my teeth out and in doing so he fell over on top of me.

While grandma was bathing my wounds I asked if I should tell the police.

'The police?' she said. 'The police? They're the biggest anti-Semites of all.'

I don't know what made me bring up the idea because I was terrified of the police myself. Jasinksi, the police chief, was a notorious anti-Semite and when I saw a policeman approaching I would cross to the other side of the road. I was particularly nervous of a stunted little officer in shiny boots whose revolver nearly reached up to his armpit and who would strut down

Pilsudskiya Ulitse as if he owned it, and even Polyna spoke of the police as hooligans.

Kowalski, the mayor, was also said to be an anti-Semite, and one heard complaints on every side about the officious and bloody-minded nature of the local bureaucracy.

All of which made me wonder why people were content to remain in Breslev and I soon discovered that a great many were not, for every Friday at assembly the headmaster would begin: 'We say farewell this week to our good friend ... who is leaving with his family for ... '

He must have covered the entire globe in the course of his farewells, America, Australia, South Africa, Palestine, the Argentine, Mexico, even China.

The people with some initiative and a little money were prepared to try their chances and start a new life in a new world. The people without were compelled to remain in place and those who weren't doing too badly, like my mother's family, with all the handicaps and hazards they were facing, preferred to stay put. They had roots, standing, sufficiency, none of which they would be assured of anywhere else.

'So they think everything is so wonderful in America?' said grandma. 'Ask Aaron Mattis.'

In the meantime I continued to explore Breslev and its environs, if only because I did not have much opportunity to do anything else, and eventually made my way to the railway station about a mile out of town.

It was a small station staffed by an old man with thick glasses, and a freckled youngster, both of them in uniform, like policemen, and served a minor narrow-gauge branch line used mainly by timber wagons which seemed to be shunted back and forward without going anywhere. About five in the evening, however, a passenger train pulled in and that was enough to make my day.

The engine was small and chunky with a long funnel and bore no relation to the great snorting monster I had seen in Dvinsk, but a passenger train in motion – even in slow-motion – was a wondrous sight to my eyes, and I returned to the station again and again, in fact every day except Friday, Saturday and Sunday. I became quite friendly with the station master and his assistant and learned more Polish from them than I had ever learned at school. If all Poles were anti-Semites I had found two exceptions.

At last I had something to look forward to, the five o'clock train, and if weekends dragged on rather wearily, there was always the thought of the five o'clock train on Monday to keep me going.

It meant, of course, that I had to skip Heder, but Heder wasn't like school. They didn't keep a register and I was so quiet and shadowy when I was there that I didn't suppose anyone would notice if I wasn't.

This continued for a month or two. Then one day my grandmother bumped into the headmaster of the Heder who asked if I had returned to Barovke, because he hadn't seen anything of me for a long time.

That evening when I returned from the station I found grandma, Chaim Kasre and the headmaster waiting for me.

I could see at a glance that the game was up. I readily confessed to my misdeeds and entered upon the darkest phase of my stay, but even then there were moments of relief.

One morning, as I was ambling along in my usual dejected fashion, I was overtaken by an attractive young woman with large blue eyes, auburn hair and a bright smile, who gave me a bar of Swiss chocolate. I still remember the cows on the wrapper and the taste of the chocolate, but have no idea who the woman was, or why she gave me the chocolate. She might have been an angel. She certainly looked like one, and the memory of the incident, to say nothing of the memory of the chocolate, sustained me for several weeks, though in subsequent years I came to wonder if she had not been conjured up by my imagination.

I never asked father for money, but – when mother wasn't looking – he would slip me the occasional kopek to buy a caramel or an ice-cream. (Kopeks and roubles were Russian coins, but whether in Latvia or Poland when it came to money we tended to think in Russian terms.) In Breslev I was moneyless. Mother sent me none, and grandmother and my uncles gave me none.

All of which might suggest they were mean, but as I could see

from the constant succession of *meshullochim* who descended on
the house they were fairly generous where charity was concerned,
and obviously believed that small children should not be spoilt.

One evening a celebrated cantor came to town and gave a
performance in the main synagogue for which he charged a fee.
Chaim Kasre was in the audience in one of the expensive seats
and looking round he found me in the next row, which was also
an expensive area.

He asked where I found the money and I said I had sneaked in,
which made him angry.

'We don't do that in Breslev. Next time you want to go to a
concert, tell me, and I'll give you the money.'

About a month later another concert was announced and he
gave me a coin which would have paid for one of the cheaper
seats. The concert, for some reason, never took place and he asked
for his money back.

I had seven first cousins in Breslev, but as they were all much
younger than me I had little or nothing to do with them, so that I
was left very much on my own and would go to any occasion
which offered the prospect of company, like synagogue on a
weekday evening. There would be a few old men about who were
always friendly and who would offer me a pinch of snuff, and one
or two youngsters might turn up to say Kaddish for their parents.

I would even tag on to funerals. The coffins were carried on foot
along the entire length of Pilsudskiya Ulitza to the cemetery, and
there was always a long procession behind them. I must have been
tall for my age, or the men were inordinately short, for I took my
turn as pall-bearer, or perhaps I swung on to the poles. It was a
mitsva (good deed), and offered company of sorts.

I also joined any street games going, where I was tolerated – I
had by then given up any hope of being actually accepted – and
one of them was a rudimentary game of tiddly-winks played with
buttons.

I asked grandma if she had any buttons to spare.

'What for?'

'To play with.'

'Buttons aren't toys.'

I then examined my Sabbath suit and discovered three buttons on each sleeve which didn't seem to be performing any useful purpose and promptly cut them off. I could join the crowd.

Unfortunately it was a game of skill and, as with all games of skill, I was a non-starter and quickly lost all six buttons, but I didn't give up. I returned to my Sabbath suit and cut off the fly buttons, and lost them as well which left me a bit exposed to the elements. (Polyna, bless her, noticed the gap – and perhaps more than the gap – and sewed on a new set. 'I can understand you losing one button,' she grumbled, 'or even two, but how could you lose all four? What have you been doing with yourself?') By then I was convinced that my luck would have to turn. I wondered whether grandma really needed all the buttons she had on her frocks, but for some reason she always kept her bedroom door locked and instead I invaded the room occupied by Chaim Kasre and his wife, and there found a virtual Aladin's cave, long dresses with buttons all the way down, and no buttonholes.

I didn't go wild, but cut a couple of buttons from one dress, a couple from another, and came away with quite a store, and again lost them all.

I dare say I would have rendered the entire household buttonless, if I hadn't been caught, but caught I was, with scissors in hand attacking a black suit with satin lapels belonging to Chaim Kasre.

'What shall I do with you?' cried grandma, literally tearing her hair. 'What shall I do with you? What will become of you? You're driving me to an early grave. Do you want me to write to your mother?'

'No.'

'To your father?'

'No.'

'Will you promise me not to touch another button?'

I promised, and began stealing money instead.

I am not sure what made me turn to outright theft, because whatever complaints I may have had about my treatment in Breslev, I was never hungry. I am not even sure that I had any serious complaints at all, because if I was largely ignored I was never neglected. I may not have been loved – except possibly by Polyna – but then I was not particularly lovable and no one away from his parents has any automatic claim to affection.

It may have been simply a matter of opportunity, for one afternoon I found grandma's handbag open in front of me, and on impulse I slipped my hand in and fished out a small silver coin. I spent it the next morning.

There is a Talmudic saying – I'm beginning to sound like my father – *aveyro goreres aveyro*, sin begets sin, and this was a classical instance of it.

The next morning happened to be the Sabbath, and I bought an almond slice – I can taste it on my tongue to this day – in a non-kosher bakery, and I thus committed three sins in one go – theft, desecration of the holy Sabbath and eating non-kosher food. And a fourth one if it comes to that, for I should have been in synagogue at the time. I was soon to commit a fifth.

I did not expect to be struck dead the moment I entered the shop on the holy Sabbath, or to choke over the almond slice – in fact I enjoyed it to the last crumb, but I was filled with apprehensions that Grandma would find me out, and if she didn't God almost certainly would.

I was familiar with the prayer: 'The Lord is merciful and gracious ... bestowing loving kindness on thousands, forgiving iniquity, transgressions and sin,' but there was a limit to the number of sins one might reasonably expect even God to forgive, especially if committed in quick succession and, when a few days later the saintly Nosson came to lunch, I pulled him aside.

I'm not sure why I importuned him. Did I hope for absolution, or was it merely a matter of curiosity about what I had let myself in for? Perhaps it was his very air of sanctity which drew me out. I was not even sure what I intended to tell him, but when I found myself looking into his large watery eyes I couldn't come clean and told him about 'a friend' who had stolen money from his grandmother and as I piled iniquity on to iniquity his eyes grew larger and larger till I was afraid they might shoot out of his head.

When I finished he stood there in silence, his hand to his mouth, swaying his head from side to side, as if absorbing the enormity of what he had just heard. Finally he said:

'But what made you do it?'

'I didn't say I did it, I said my friend – '

'Don't say another word,' he screamed, 'please, not another word, you're only adding to your sins.'

I expected chastisement, the threat of hell-fire and damnation, but he calmed down, asked for my name and my father's name, and said that he would pray for me.

It was, I suppose, an absolution of sorts, but I came to be sorry that I had broached the matter at all for that was the last I saw of him and can only presume that he no longer regarded grandma's table as kosher, and as he wasn't replaced by anyone else the poor woman may even have been black-listed.

Nor did the exchange lead me to mend my ways, for as I wasn't caught I continued to dip into grandmother's handbag and various pockets at various intervals. The sums were small, enough to buy a cake here, some sweets there, but if I suffered from anything it was not so much pangs of conscience, as the fear of being found out. Every day, on the way home from school, I braced myself for a confrontation with grandma, or even the police, for it was one thing to steal buttons, and quite another to steal money, but the money I stole was never missed – which suggested to my mind that grandma was, indeed, rich – and I was never caught.

I occasionally asked myself whether the pleasure I got from the confections was equal to the fear of discovery, for the one was momentary, while the other hovered over me like a dark cloud for days on end, but I was such a glutton that I also derived pleasure from anticipation and in retrospect, I sometimes wonder if it wasn't my gluttony which kept me going. In any case I could no longer help myself.

Which doesn't mean to say that I became a kleptomaniac. There was every opportunity for rifling pockets in the school cloakroom, but I was never tempted to do so. I only stole from the family – possibly in the belief that what was theirs was also mine – and only widened my horizons when we moved to Glasgow and I began stealing from Woolworths (but then so did everybody else). I finally abandoned the habit when I was about 14, and if I don't know what made me start, I don't know what made me stop, though it was just as well I did stop for if I had continued any longer I might have turned professional.

There are very few occasions in the Jewish calendar for actual merrymaking, and one of them, as I have explained, is Purim. The school staged an annual play for the event and I was given a small part as one of the wise men in the court of Ahasuerus. Things, I felt, were finally beginning to look up for me, for timid and shy though I was, I loved dressing up and performing, and in the course of rehearsal displayed such talents as to take both the teacher and cast by surprise. They had suddenly become aware of my presence.

We were all required to supply our own costumes, and Polyna told me that there was still a costume which my uncle Rachmiel had used for a Purim play in a box in the basement.

I immediately rushed down to try it on, slipped on the stairs, and fell head first on to the concrete floor. Hearing the noise from the courtyard, grandma rushed into the basement and found me motionless in a pool of blood.

'*Der kind is teit*,' she cried, the child is dead, and nearly died herself.

Polyna appeared just then, and so did several men from the granary. She bathed my wound, while someone rushed out for a doctor.

I had cracked my skull and had lost a considerable quantity of blood, but the doctor was able to patch me up without much difficulty and my main worry, as I came to, was that I would be missing the Purim play.

The next day, however, I developed a very high fever. Psalms were said for me in synagogue and my uncle Rachmiel was dispatched to fetch mother from Barovke, but there was some sort of international crisis and all the borders were closed, which was just as well, for I soon recovered, but missed the Purim play. I still have a dent in my skull as a souvenir of the incident.

My Polish exile was drawing to a close. My mother and sisters were due to join us for Passover after which we would all be returning to Barovke to prepare for our departure to Glasgow, but it looked for a time as if our plans might be disrupted.

I sensed something momentous was going to happen when I stood on the hill one blustery Sunday afternoon and noticed a great deal of activity in the station, with one train in the siding and another by the platform at a time of day when there were usually no trains at all. I rushed down to see what was happening, but was prevented from going anywhere near the station by a soldier in uniform with an actual gun in his hand.

That night I was wakened by the rumble of lorries whose headlights, shining through cracks in the shutters, kept lighting up my room and I hardly slept a wink.

The next day military police banned all traffic from the main street while heavily armed soldiers, some on horseback, some in lorries, but mostly on foot, moved through the town, not in neat formation or regular order, no clop, clop, clop on the cobbles like soldiers on parade, but in endless lines and at normal walking pace.

They said it was spring manoeuvres but, as someone pointed out, frontiers weren't usually closed during manoeuvres, but they were all closed and nothing could move out of Breslev nor into it.

I saw my first plane, or rather planes, six of them – bi-planes – flying in close formation, a wondrous sight. I sensed the anxieties in the faces and voices around me.

If there was a word I used to hear more than any other it was *milchomo, krieg, voyna* – war – but it was always of wars past. Now there seemed to be a new war in prospect and I found it all marvellously exciting. I was too stupid to understand the full implications of war, or possibly welcomed the prospect of a diversion whatever its form, but I was finally beginning to enjoy Breslev.

All talk everywhere was of the crisis. I presumed it all had something to do with Hitler but the causes turned out to be more local. Poland had grabbed a large chunk of Lithuania – including the capital Vilnius – some 15 years earlier. The Lithuanians were clamouring to get it back and had massed troops on the frontier.

'Where will it end, where will it end?' grandma kept asking.

'First the Great War, then the Revolution, then the Civil War, the war with Russia, the war with Lithuania, and now another war. You don't get a chance to breathe.'

The crisis, however, soon eased, and a few days later the long lines of troops, first the infantry, then the cavalry and finally the lorries, began moving in an opposite direction. The borders re-opened and one afternoon I returned from school and found mother having tea with grandma.

I had expected her to jump to her feet and rush towards me with open arms. Instead she put her hands to her cheeks, looked at me open mouthed, and turned on grandma:

'*Vos host du geton tsu mayne kind? Er zet oys shreklesh.*' What have you done to my child? He looks ghastly.

I was dumbfounded, not at her words, but at the fact that she could have raised her voice to her own mother. Poor grandma was visibly shattered.

My three sisters soon appeared and things calmed down, but I became aware that the relationship between my mother and hers and mother and her siblings was not an easy one. I was unaware of the cause of the tensions but they may explain why I was received in Breslev with less than enthusiasm, though given the anxieties I had caused, I may have been the source of the tensions.

Passover, normally the most joyous occasion of the year, came about a week later. There were about 20 of us round the table in grandma's salon for the first night of the festival, including aunt Leika, Welfke and their two small children; Chaim Kasre, his wife and her father, a large, silent man with cataracts in both eyes; and Rachmiel and his wife to be, pretty, petite, with bright eyes, a dazzling smile and a determined little chin. Polyna, in a spotless white apron, had brought over two young nieces to serve at table.

Grandma had brought out her best silver and gleaming crystal for the event, and we had actual wine in our cups instead of the usual mead we drank on Passover in Barovke, but for all the splendour of the setting and the richness of the fare, and the excited shrieks of the children, it was a subdued affair. Many of the women were in tears for much of the time and Leika wept uncontrollably (as she often did).

None of us anticipated what lay ahead, but in those days if someone went to live abroad – if only as far as England – there was a general presumption that one would not see them again.

We certainly did not expect to see grandma again, though she could not have been more than 58. She had aged visibly during my nine months in Breslev, and I was probably the principal cause of her ageing. She looked old when I came, but formidable. She now looked old and frail. She was white-haired, careworn and had lost the sight of one eye, and the pearls she wore round her long neck merely highlighted the signs of age.

I had warmed to her during my last weeks in Breslev, not because she had warmed to me, but because I had begun to understand her.

As we left Breslev we passed by the Jewish cemetery and came upon the most tragic sight of my young life. There was a girl of about 12 or 13 crying over a grave. It was not unusual to see people crying over graves, but she was so young and was crying at the top of her voice, as if her heart might break and I asked grandma who she was.

Her parents and siblings had emigrated to America and because she was slightly backward she had been left behind with her grandmother. Her grandmother had died a month later and she was now on her own.

Chapter 11

Final Exit

Barovke wasn't the same after my nine months away, and I don't suppose I was either.

For a start father was no longer around. I had got used to being fatherless in Poland but then I had also been motherless in Poland, and friendless. It was odd to be back to a familiar place with the most familiar element in it missing, and a father in Glasgow was almost as remote as Father in Heaven.

It was also odd to go into synagogue and find father's place by the ark empty. The synagogue no longer looked like a synagogue, it felt vaguely deconsecrated. This was particularly the case with the small synagogue which – when he wasn't preaching – was his favourite of the two. It was not that he thought that small was beautiful, but it was more cosy, compact, snug and the favourite resort of his closest cronies. Father had his critics in the main synagogue, but only devotees in the small one and he had no doubt that given the choice the divine presence would have alighted on the latter rather than the former. The small synagogue sans father seemed not only small, but desolate – a cheerless, airless, decrepit little hovel.

In Breslev a great many people seemed to be sitting on their cases waiting for a visa, a paper, a ticket to go somewhere, anywhere, and one could sense menace in the very air. Barovke was not like that, but it was no longer at ease. Perhaps it never was and I had merely become more mature and sensitive to the mood around me, but everyone envied us, not because we were moving from a small *shtetaleh* to a big *shtot*, but because we were getting out, not only out of Latvia but, so to speak, out of Europe, though some wondered why, since we were moving, we didn't make for America – as if we had any say in the matter.

America, in the Jewish imagination, was still *die golderneh medineh*, the golden land. England, at best, was the silver one, but silver or not it had a lot to commend it, and when I returned to Barovke it seemed to be on everybody's lips.

In the course of my three years' schooling I had not learned all that much history, and even less geography. The little we learned was, understandably, about eastern Europe rather than the west, and I had heard of England mainly as the home of chocolate, shoes and *shtoff* – men's clothing material. Also, until the rise of Hitler, there was the general feeling that the further west one went the better it was for the Jews, so that Germany was better than Latvia, France was better than Germany, and England was better still, so that I had a vague idea where it was situated. I was also aware that it governed Palestine, so that it featured prominently – and not always favourably – in the Yiddish press.

At school in Barovke we had a new teacher with a middle parting, wing-collar and waxed moustache, who claimed to know English and when he heard I was moving to Glasgow he moved me to the front seat and tried out what he knew on me.

'Gut morning, how are you? – and what do you say?'

I had no idea.

'Ferry fell tenk you. What do you say?'

'Ferry fell tenk you.'

After which he would greet me with 'gut morning, how are you?' every morning and 'ferry fell tenk you' were the first English words I learned.

He also gave us a lesson in recent history. The 'English' – he never used the word British and had probably never heard of it – had apparently helped Latvia to gain her independence, so that as a prospective Englishman, I was suddenly regarded as something of a hero by my classmates.

England also came up in conversation in the naked forum on Friday afternoons.

'Hitler wants this, Hitler wants that, Hitler wants everything,' said Beirach, 'but England stopped the Kaiser, and they'll stop Hitler.'

As a result I naturally gloried in my prospective status until Shaike took the trouble to point England out on the map, and it seemed so small, especially compared to America that I couldn't understand what the fuss was about. It was hardly bigger than Latvia, which was a bit of a letdown and I couldn't understand what a small country on the edge of Europe could be doing in Palestine.

In the meantime Barovke itself was shrinking. People had enjoyed something like stability for a mere 15 years after prolonged periods of chaos, and now the clouds were darkening once again. We were leaving because we were not allowed to stay, others began to leave because they felt it was unsafe to stay and were doing so quietly, almost furtively, as if nervous of causing a panic. Chatskel-and-his-six-sons, to say nothing of his wife and daughter, vanished suddenly like thieves in the night, and it was rumoured that Shmuel Trupin was looking for a buyer for his meat company.

When father left he was not replaced by another rabbi, either because they couldn't find one, or couldn't afford one, and they brought in a young man with large glasses and a young wife, who acted as *shochet* and teacher, but there was nothing in his appearance to suggest the semi-ecclesiastical nature of his calling. Where father was bearded, he was cleanshaven. Father wore a long coat, he wore a short jacket and, instead of a high-crowned beaver hat, he wore a straw hat and carried a bamboo stick. In fact he was something of a dandy. He came from Dvinsk and it was said that his wife had money.

There was, of course, speculation as to why anyone with money from a *shtot* like Dvinsk should want to settle in a *shtetaleh* like Barovke.

It soon emerged that apart from being a *shochet* he had also been a *mohel*, a circumcizer, and had moved to Barovke after suffering a mishap. Such mishaps were not uncommon, as one could see from a visit to the bath-house, but it must have been a considerable mishap for he never functioned as a *mohel* in Barovke.

He and his wife had been married for some years, but they were still childless, which provoked further speculation, and Zamke, who was a minor authority on a host of improbable subjects, let it be known that he used a 'rubber cap'. He did not explain why he used it, or how, and backward as ever in such matters, I presumed he wore it on his head.

Father used to teach the older boys in Heder, while Moshe Yudeh took the younger ones. Moshe Yudeh had, however, been laid low by some mysterious illness and the new man took all the classes. Encountered in the street he looked smiling and amiable, even urbane, but he was a different man once he stood before the class and ruled us literally with a rod of iron – a device made out of wrought wire which looked like the handle of a carpet beater.

Our parents believed in, and were practitioners of, corporal punishment but a rod of iron was too much even for them, and though the new man protested that he only flourished the instrument as a deterrent, he was compelled to abandon it.

Personally, I could have lived with the rod of iron. What I couldn't take was the other novelty he had introduced, *dik-duk*, which sounds like a game, but which is actually Hebrew grammar.

Father had taken his classes through Scripture with all the major commentaries, and on to the foothills of the Talmud in the belief that once a boy became familiar with the sacred texts his understanding of grammar would fall into place of its own accord. He had learned none and was disposed to teach none. This man, on the contrary, believed that once you knew grammar, you would find no difficulty in grasping anything else, but I found it impossible to grasp grammar at all.

I had encountered the same problem at the Yavneh school in Breslev, but Yavneh was at least a day school and they taught Hebrew grammar much in the way that they taught Polish grammar (which I had also failed to grasp, and I have not even grasped English grammar), but I never expected that I would have to face it in Heder. There was something mildly un-Jewish about the whole idea and, after about a month of endless boredom and fruitless effort, I added to the number of my accomplishments by forging a letter from mother asking to be excused further attendance at Heder because we were preparing to leave for Glasgow.

And again it was not a complete fabrication because we were making almost weekly visits to Dvinsk for new clothes – not even Moishe Zeitlin's emporium could fit us out properly for our new life in Glasgow.

Mother acquired a black fur coat with a magnificent cape and a fur hat, and my sisters elegant frocks, while I was kitted out with a set of plus-fours made of English cloth. The first time I had seen such an outfit before, it was worn by a German *graf* on a shooting expedition to the neighbourhood. I felt a bit like a *graf* myself.

I was nine by then and tall for my age and, if not quite on the brink of manhood, mother felt that I had outgrown my childish clothes. I also had a new hat fashioned out of the same material as my suit.

'*A gantser mentsch*' – a complete man – she said when my ensemble was complete and unusually for her, she gave me a warm embrace.

She was in a buoyant mood. She was enjoying what was, for her, a prolonged spell of good health, possibly because she was too busy to have time for ill-health, or because she wasn't having any miscarriages. We were no longer hard-pressed financially and we were about to exchange life in the *shtetaleh* for life in the *shtot* where, she was confident, she would be among people of her class.

She may also have enjoyed the remission from being a *rebbetzin* – a rabbi's wife. The role of *rebbetzin* in eastern Europe carried considerable status but no formal responsibilities. It did, however, place her in the public eye, which carried obvious restraints, and she had to be on her best behaviour. Not that she was ever – to my knowledge – inclined to misbehave, but now that father was gone and the aura of sanctity had been removed from our household she may have felt less inhibited. At all events she became more womanly. The fact that she had more money may also have had something to do with it because I saw objects round the house that I hadn't seen before, like face cream, hand cream, lipstick and perfume sprays. Perhaps she had always had them, but now used them more frequently, for she smelt differently.

If my mother did give me greater attention than my sisters, it was partly because in spite of my love of display, I was slovenly in habit – as I still am – and she was at pains to tidy me up in case I should be a source of embarrassment. Moreover, as a *ben-yochid*, an only son, I was richly entitled to special attention.

I only wore the plus-fours once while in Latvia, and that was to pose for a family photo, after which it was carefully packed away for my new life in Glasgow where, I presumed, everyone wore plus-fours. However, I suspect that mother did not want me to wear them in Barovke, not because I might stain or crumple them – which I probably would – but because someone might give me an *ayin hora*.

By the time I was seven or eight my father had sadly concluded that I lacked the necessary aptitude or intelligence to be a rabbi and, after he settled in Glasgow, he suggested that I might want to become a doctor, which was well beyond my own level of aspirations, or even dreams.

'In Glasgow,' he wrote, 'everything is possible,' and every letter he wrote enlarged on the wonders of the place:

'They eat four meals a day whether they're hungry or not ... '

'They eat meat and fish even on weekdays and sometimes in the same meal ... '

'Every house has a bath, and some people bathe every day whether they're dirty or clean ... '

'All the *goyim* are friendly and hardly any of them are drunk ... ' (which, coming from Glasgow, suggests that he couldn't have been looking very hard).

'Every *shlepper* has a phone and some even have automobiles ... '

'People dress on weekdays as if it was Shabbos ... '

'The streets are all lit at night with lights so bright, you can read by them ... '

'There are libraries where they lend you books – even Yiddish books – for nothing, and trust you to bring them back … '

'There are parks and gardens all over town which stretch as far as the eye can see, with swings and roundabouts, and they're all free … '

'Even the Jews have dogs, but they don't bite, and hardly even bark … '

'There are no wooden houses in Glasgow. Everyone lives in stone towers which reach up to the skies … '

He eventually sent us a photo of 'the stone tower' in which we would be living, four storeys high, and which indeed looked as if it might reach to the skies.

Mother read out the wonders to us and I reread them to my assembled friends; but for the photograph of the actual building they would not have believed me. I did not add that we would only be occupying one flat in the building – and, as it turned out, a small one, at that – but not telling the whole truth was not quite the same as telling a lie.

Not that I hesitated to tell lies if the occasion demanded – or even if it didn't. Some of my friends had been to Dvinsk, but I alone among them had crossed an actual frontier and felt obliged to describe the marvels which lay beyond, even when I had not actually witnessed them.

I may not have been particularly good at lying my way out of a scrape, but when it came to complete fabrication I was tops. Indeed I was so good that I wasn't always certain myself whether I was telling a lie or not, and it may have been the source of my subsequent career as an author.

And thus I described one trip to Vilno and another to Warsaw. And when they asked how I got there I had to describe the train journey, which I did in great detail, even though I had never actually set foot on a train.

'Did they have sleeping-wagons?'

'Sleeping wagons?'

'You know, wagons in which you can sleep.'

'Oh yes, with beds and *perines*, and hot tea from samovars.' (A description which, as I later discovered, turned out to be accurate.)

Once you start lying, there's no end to it. A good liar needs a good memory and my memory in those days was faultless and I was never caught out. Previously I may have been crown prince of Barovke by virtue of being my father's son. Now I was something of a king among my contemporaries in my own right.

Mother, with the fiver she received monthly from father now gave me regular pocket money, not a lot but enough to have actual coins jingling in my pockets, a novel and reassuring sound, and I was able to treat my friends, who grew in number by the day, to sweets and caramels. I even bought a bar of Five Boys English chocolate from Moishe Zeitlins, which, of course, I shared. I was not only rich but generous.

With Leipkaleh in Riga I was made number three in the gang, and could thus march at the head of the column, which, however, was depleted in length, and I no longer had the same awe for our commander Zamke Zussman. He seemed to have shrunk and did not exude the same air of authority, though Shaike was every bit as exotic as he used to be. His mother looked even more exotic and when she was around I became conscious of stirrings within myself which I had not experienced before.

I still said my bedtime prayers and would settle into sleep with the thought of Michael at my right hand, Gabriel at my left, Uriel before me and Raphael behind me, but instead of having the divine presence of God above my head, I tended to see Shaike's mother.

Leipkaleh the great came home on holiday. He had hardly grown in size but was totally transformed in appearance, for he had long hair like Shaike, but parted in the middle and, though it was high summer, he wore long trousers, sandals and socks – but not plus-fours.

He did not spend much time with Zamke or the rest, and regarded the whole gang with disdain.

'It's about time they grew up,' he said, but he had a long chat with me like one man of the world addressing another.

I was flattered by his attention but was upset by the way he dismissed everyone and everything in Barovke. 'Who are they? What are they? *Nebbichs*, all of them. If they wouldn't be *nebbichs* they wouldn't be here.'

'Boruch Sholem, a *nebbich*?'

'A rich *nebbich*.'

'Abrasha Pinchashowits a *nebbich*?'

'Spends most of his time in Riga.'

He was making the small world in which I had finally begun to triumph even smaller, though he was in fact confirming an impression that I was beginning to form myself.

I was curious to know what he thought of father who had spent endless hours giving him private tuition without fee, but I was nervous of asking, and though he often inquired about him and said how much he liked him, he never ventured an opinion of him.

My mother, in the meantime, was able to give full reign to the pronounced entrepreneurial instincts which had been largely dormant since the day she married, and let it be known that everything in our house, other than me and my sisters – and I half suspect she would have sold us too if she got the right price – was for sale.

We had returned to Barovke at the end of April and were due to leave for Glasgow in July and, for a start, she disposed of our winter underwear, woollen *kaftels* so thick and heavy that they could have served as suits of armour, and old and frayed though they were she managed to find a buyer.

She then sold our chickens together with her old clothes, including her *wolikes*, in one job lot to Nehama the bath-attendant.

Finally, she turned to the house, or rather on the house. By the end of May, we had no curtains, no tablecloths and no pots and pans, and borrowed some from our neighbour, Bashke Ratz. By the beginning of June, we no longer had our cutlery and crockery, and borrowed some from her daughter-in-law, Hannah Ratz.

By the middle of June, we had no beds or bedding. I can't remember where my mother or sisters slept, but I shared a bed over the road with Hannah Ratz's son, a five-year-old who wet his bed every night – the little bastard did it on purpose because I could hear him sniggering under his sheets.

For a week or so we ate different meals in different homes, like wandering paupers, though it gave us an opportunity to say our farewells.

One evening it was with Shimshon Ber. His daughter, old, bent and deaf, was an uncommonly bad cook who served uncommonly large portions, and I half choked with every mouthful I swallowed.

It was mainly a gathering of father's old Talmud crowd, now a little depleted because Mendel der schwarter had emigrated and Mendel der geller was dead, though by way of compensation Binyomin Rosin had brought along his son-in-law, Yankel, who closed the evening with a performance of 'The Carnival of Venice' on his trumpet ('The Last Post' would have been more appropriate).

Old Shimshon Ber was in tears.

'At my age I can't hope to see anyone again. Barovke isn't Barovke without Reb Azriel. The glory has gone out of Zion.'

'We didn't deserve Reb Azriel,' said Beirach. 'I only hope Glasgow does.'

Boruch Sholem made a meal like a wedding banquet and had a dozen guests round his table, including Abrasha Pinchashowits and his wife.

No tears this time and the tributes were addressed to mother rather than father. Mother, in a brown satin dress with a velvet bodice and neatly corrugated hair, looked striking. 'She brought the flavour of the *shtot* to our *shtetl*,' said Pinchashowits. 'Barovke will seem very small without her.' His wife asked mother for the name of her dressmaker.

Shmuel Trupin made another banquet, also with about a dozen guests. Mother was there in the same satin dress and all but outshone Soreleh. I wondered if Shaike felt about my mother the way I felt about his. As a farewell present, Trupin gave us six sticks of his best *wursht*.

'They'll last for ever,' he said, and they did, though by the time we got round to using them we had to cut them with a hacksaw.

And finally there was Chaim Ratz, who also had a large gathering, but served a small meal.

The guests included Moishe Yudeh and his wife Raizel who arrived squawking, left squawking and continued to squawk throughout the meal.

'You're going, everyone's going, I wish we could go.'

'I'm not going,' said Ratz.

'At your age there's only one place you can go. It's the same with us. Who'd have us with him half crippled and me half dead, and my legs so swollen I can hardly get my stockings on. And in any case what's the point of going? You find anti-Semites everywhere, a curse on them.'

Titania could not invite us to a meal because of dietary problems but arranged a sort of tea party, and she and mother spent half the evening crying on each other's shoulders.

I had been looking forward to our great move to Glasgow with the keenest anticipation for it had begun to feature in my imagination as another New York, a place full of wonders, and father had promised me the bicycle. Above all, there was the thought of seeing father himself.

There was also the prospect of the railway journey, not on one of those short, tinny, toy trains I had seen in Breslev, but on one of those long, massive expresses with their great thundering locomotives which I had seen in Dvinsk. Shaike and Leipkaleh had been on a train from Dvinsk to Riga, but I would be travelling from one end of Europe to the other, with a sea crossing at the end of it – and I had not even seen the sea. It was almost more than my imagination could embrace. Yet as the day of departure drew near I was seized with a mass of conflicting emotions.

While describing the wonders of Glasgow, father had said nothing about lakes or forests, mills, mill ponds or mill streams, or wild strawberries.

Summer came early that year and, as one cloudless day succeeded another, Barovke with its small homes and small gardens, green meadows, fruit-laden orchards, gleaming waters, dusty footpaths, tethered goats, and great open skies, never looked more enchanting. I could see what I was giving up, but only had a hazy and shifting picture of what I might be acquiring.

I missed father but was not entirely sorry to be liberated from the chore of daily lessons, especially in May and June, when they were largely concerned with animal sacrifices and entrails and priestly accoutrements. I was therefore free to play with the gang in the evening, to join them in games at the back of the synagogue on the Sabbath, to be a boy like other boys. It was good to be desanctified and returning to father would mean returning to divine supervision.

My sojourn in Breslev made me nervous of what the future might hold for me in Glasgow. To be sure I would have my parents and sisters around me, but there was no telling how I would be received by my peers. Here I was surrounded by friends and companions and was somebody at last. The chances were that in Glasgow I would be nobody.

I therefore threw myself into that last summer with a gusto I had never displayed before, as if to make sure that, if nothing else, I would have vivid memories to feed on. We went fishing in the mill stream – using old knickers as nets – and grilled our fish on open fires. We raided orchards and half poisoned ourselves with half-ripe fruit. We feasted on wild strawberries. We went dunking in the mill pond and swimming in the lake. We penetrated the forest as far as the Polish border, and were turned back by armed frontier guards.

Then our tickets arrived in the form of a voluminous booklet with the name Thos. Cook and Sons in large letters on the yellow covers. I leafed through the pages with shaking hands – Riga, Kaunas, Berlin, Cologne, Brussels, Ostend, Dover, London, Glasgow. The die was cast, our Barovke days were over.

But not quite. Some sort of hitch had occurred, mother went into hysterics, and Sonja, whom father had entrusted with overseeing our travel arrangements, arrived from Dvinsk to calm her down and sort things out. There were hurried meetings with Jan the policeman and Pinchashovits the lawyer, and anxious phone calls, and within 24 hours everything was in order. I didn't know whether to cheer or cry.

The day finally dawned. We had been up much of the night making last-minute preparations and, even with all my invocations to Michael, Raphael and the rest, I was far too excited to fall asleep. I was more asleep than awake as we staggered up the hill to the cobbled square for the morning bus.

The bus left at six but early though it was, the gang were all there, Zamke, Shaike, Leipkaleh, Welfke, Shmulke and the rest and they too looked half asleep.

Normally when together we all talked at once and Zamke had to bawl at the top of his voice to impose order. Now we were all tongue-tied. Zamke was the first to find his voice.

'You won't forget to write.'

'Write?'

'Letters.'

'Oh yes, every week.'

'No, you won't,' said Leipkaleh. 'you'll forget you ever knew us.'

Several of my sisters' friends, including Marintsa, had also turned up and there was much kissing and hugging and not a few tears as the bus pulled up. Marintsa also gave me a kiss and a hug, which was the first time I had been kissed and hugged by a non-relative. It was a delightful sensation, which made me all the more sorry that I was leaving.

I shook hands with each of my friends like a commander saying farewell to his guard and vaulted up the steps of the bus.

I did not look back till the bus pulled out, and they looked small and forlorn as they stood there waving their hands in the morning mist.

Epilogue

When war broke out in September 1939 I had a grandfather, an uncle, two aunts and five cousins living in Latvia, and a grandmother, four uncles, four aunts and eight cousins living in Poland, 26 souls in all. Only two survived. One fell in battle. The other 23 were slaughtered by the Nazis and their allies.

When we said our last farewells in 1938 we were fairly certain that we would never see our relatives again if only because, in those days, such partings by their very nature tended to be fairly permanent. The fact that war clouds were once again gathering over Europe did not enter into consideration because my parents had rarely lived under clear skies. Life in eastern Europe was a struggle for stability in an atmosphere of crisis.

We corresponded regularly with grandma in Breslev, grandpa in Kreslavka, and Sonja in Dvinsk and received occasional letters from various uncles and aunts. Once the fighting began on 1 September 1939, we heard nothing more from Poland, even though Breslev was in the Russian zone, but we took no news to be good news. Stalin, after all, wasn't Hitler and the Communists weren't Nazis.

One of the few Jewish survivors of those war years recalls that the Jews of Breslev 'welcomed the Red Army with great joy, with flowers, bread and salt', while a local draper, Aharon Zeif, distributed rolls of red cloth for the manufacture of Russian flags.

The joy proved to be short-lived as the Jewish religious and cultural institutions were closed down and the study of Hebrew and even Yiddish were banned.

We continued to get letters sporadically from Latvia – I believe they came via Sweden – and then they too stopped.

In July 1940 Latvia was absorbed by the Soviet Union, which father also thought was good news of sorts, for there were fears that it might be absorbed by Germany.

On 22 June 1941, the Germans attacked on the eastern front and overran the Baltic states and the Russian zone of Poland within days. They were in Barovke by 26 June, Breslev on 28 June and Kreslavka on 1 July.

My parents received the news of the German advance with the darkest foreboding, but nothing they had experienced and nothing they could imagine prepared them for what actually followed.

A Latvian, who was eight at the time, told me what happened in Barovke:

'The Germans went from house to house rounding up Jews, men, women, young, old, marched them to the forest and bang, bang, bang. It was all over in minutes.'

Kreslavka, as a border town, was overwhelmed with Jewish refugees within days of the German attack, all of them desperate to cross into Russia. The border was, however, closed, and they were given shelter in private houses and the local synagogues. A few days later the borders opened and about 200 Jews, including my cousin Miriam, managed to get away. A few others found shelter with Christian families in the surrounding countryside. On 28 August, several hundred Jews were marched to the edge of the town by the Germans and their Latvian auxiliaries and slaughtered. Others were transferred to the Dvinsk ghetto where they met a similar fate some two months later. My grandfather and his wife were presumably among the victims.

The agony of Breslev was more extended. When news of the German attack reached the town, a mass meeting was held on the shores of the large lake and people were assured by Communist Party officials that the Germans were being held and would be repulsed and that there was nothing to fear.

Some hours later they drew reassurance from the rumble of endless columns of Russian tanks, artillery and infantry moving towards the west. By the next day they were moving in some disarray in the opposite direction. Their dejected appearance spoke for itself. Party officials and their families were among the first to leave and many Jews prepared to follow them.

My uncle Chaim Kasre, who was one of the lay leaders of the community, said there was no need to panic.

'What is there to be afraid of?' he asked. 'They're Germans, what can they do to us?'

The area had been under German occupation during the First World War, and the Germans had behaved so benignly that the Jews came to think of them almost as liberators. Life wasn't easy, but they had introduced a degree of stability and order they had not known under Russian rule, and my uncle's argument proved sadly persuasive.

The first Germans to enter the town were intelligence men on motor cycles. There was nothing menacing about their appearance or manner; they looked around, stayed a while and left.

The next day the German army arrived in force and thundered through the town in an endless column – tanks, artillery, motorized infantry – and continued towards Vitebsk, leaving behind a small military contingent which almost immediately launched a reign of terror.

On 3 July, they rounded up all Jews and marched them at gunpoint to the swamp on the edge of the Dubkes forest where they were kept all night. Two people who fell out of line were shot on the spot.

There seemed to be no point in the whole exercise and they were allowed to leave the next morning. But, when they returned to their homes, they found that most of them had been looted by their Polish neighbours and that anything that could not be moved had been destroyed.

A few weeks later there was a Russian air attack on the vicinity.

A Pole said that he had seen a group of Jews signalling to the Russian planes and two of the accused were immediately hanged. One of them was mother's cousin, Beilka Daets. She was a small, sweet woman in her early thirties.

There were some 3,000 Jews in Breslev when we left in 1938. The Russians deported a number of the more prosperous families – including the lawyer Gilliskofsky and his wife – to central Asia, and others had left of their own accord so that by June 1941 the numbers had declined to about 2,500. The Germans, however, herded Jews from Opsa, Druya Dubene, Vidz, Okmienitz and other surrounding *shtetlech* into the town, so that the Jewish population almost doubled in size. In April 1942, they cordoned off all the side streets of Pilsudzkiya Ulitza with barbed wire and formed it into a ghetto. My grandmother's house was at the centre of it.

There had been sporadic murders from the day the Germans marched in. On 3 June 1942, the slaughter began in earnest and continued for three days. Nearly 3,000 Jews were gunned down and their bodies thrown into a large pit. The pit continued to ooze blood for the better part of a week. 'The ground seemed to heave,' said a survivor, and they had to bring in sand from the shore to cover it.

The young and able bodied still survived and in the autumn of 1942 the ghetto was converted into a labour camp. In March 1943, the Nazis began to liquidate the camp. This time they were met with armed resistance but, with few guns and little ammunition, the Jews could not hold out for long. About a dozen were able to flee to the nearby forests and join up with the partisans. The rest were wiped out.

One of the most melancholy aspects of the whole tragic story was the extent to which Latvians, Poles, Belorussians and Russians not only pillaged their Jewish neighbours, but joined enthusiastically in their slaughter. 'I can understand why they should have been prepared to rob us,' a survivor said to me, 'after all they had a free hand, but why should they have wanted to murder us? Some of them were worse than the Nazis.' The collaborators included Jasinski, the Polish chief of police, and Kowalski, the mayor.

Against which one can put the testimony of other survivors who recalled numerous people who risked their own lives to save them from the Nazis.

Darkness and Desolation, the memorial volume published by the association of Breslev survivors, lists more than 80 such individuals, including Stanislaw Szakiel who, over a period of more than two years, hid and fed 17 Jews; and several priests who, in sheltering Jews, endangered not only themselves but their communities. The Germans had few compunctions about slaughtering Poles or Russians.

One man, Leiser Fiszer, who had been mowed down in the April 1942 massacre and left for dead, managed to crawl out of the pit. For three days he wandered through the forests blood-stained, naked and famished until he found shelter near the tiny village of Zwirble with Jusef Orlowski, who kept him hidden for two years. When the other villagers became aware of Fiszer's presence, Orlowski dug a pit beneath his pigsty, and kept him hidden for a further eight months.

Perhaps the most heroic figure in Breslev, and certainly the best known, was Alexei Wasilewski, the son of the local Russian Orthodox priest who held a position of trust on the town council and who supplied the Jews with arms. He was later betrayed by a fellow Russian and shot.

The scale of the heroism did not approach the scale of the villainy, but then it never does. The non-Jewish population of Breslev and its surrounding *shtetlech* could not have been more than 10,000 so that 80 heroes, most of whom were heads of families, represented an impressive total.

Of my mother's family, only one aunt, a short, spirited and attractive young woman called Bashke, survived. She was the wife of my mother's youngest brother, Rachmiel.

Grandma had been opposed to their marriage because she was not of 'good family', whatever that meant, and because she was a *frie* and a *linke*. She was in fact a communist but, as the party was outlawed in prewar Poland, she was fairly discreet about it until the Russians occupied the town. Rachmiel was likewise a communist, though from what I remember of him, he conformed to most Jewish traditions and would accompany me regularly to synagogue on Saturday mornings. He was fairly taciturn and about the only thing he had to say to me on our walks there and back was: 'So how do you like Breslev?' and the only answer I could honestly give was that I liked Barovke better.

He joined the Red Army shortly after he married and was killed in battle in 1943. It is strange what comfort one draws from such a fact. If only my other uncles had died in the same way, but they were too old for military service.

His wife moved to Moscow and after the war we heard that she had become a fairly senior party official. She made no attempt to contact us. We tried to send her letters through various intermediaries, but she either failed to receive them or preferred not to answer them.

The rest of the family all perished in Breslev. The first account which I received from a survivor was that the family were hiding in the basement of grandma's house – the same basement in which I was nearly killed – when the Germans rolled some hand grenades down the steps and blew the place up on top of them, which is the version of events I described in my book *Coming Home*. When I visited Breslev in 1990, however, I found that the house was still standing. It was by then the home of three families, all of them Russian, all of them newcomers, who knew nothing of prewar Breslev. I have since been told that Rachel, Chaim Kasre's daughter, who was then six, was shot dead while playing in the street outside her home. Everyone else was slaughtered in June 1942.

My main source of information on Breslev is Malka, a second cousin of mother's. She was 14 at the time of the invasion and fled on foot the day the Germans reached Breslev. She then made her way across Russia to Alma Ata in central Asia and trained as a doctor. She returned to Breslev in 1949 where she met up with Moshe Milutin, a friend of the family, also from Breslev, who had escaped to the forests and had fought with the partisans. He was also involved in settling accounts with Polish collaborators once the Nazis withdrew. They married and a few years later they moved to Israel. They now live in Petach Tikva and have three children and five grandchildren. Life goes on.

There were only two survivors from father's family, a niece called Miriam who, if still alive, would now be about 75, and his cousin Sonia.

Miriam became a scientist and we heard from her two or three years after the war. She was living in Moscow by then and father tried to persuade her to come over to Glasgow. Mother was aghast at the idea because things at home were far from happy, but in any case nothing came of it. Miriam was not free to move, it was by no means clear that she wished to do so and, by the time father died in 1962, the correspondence between us, always erratic, finally petered out.

I was in Moscow in 1972 and tried to contact her. A voice answered and I explained in Yiddish who I was and asked whether I was talking to Miriam Bermant.

'Miriam Bermant isn't here,' the voice replied – again in Yiddish – 'but please do not call again.'

Sonia, though a communist, had, for some reason fallen foul of the Soviet authorities and had been deported to central Asia in June 1941, a few days before the German invasion. We don't know what happened to her husband and children but, according to Miriam, she had been allowed to return to Latvia. Our letters to her remained unanswered and she made no attempt to contact us.

A simple black obelisk marks the scene of the massacre of Barovke, and a few dried flowers at its foot suggested recent visitors.

I have seen many such memorials, but know of none more poignant, not only because I knew and loved the people involved, but because of the lakeside setting, the silence of the surrounding forest and the soft, insistent lapping of the water. The 23rd Psalm inevitably came to mind when I was there in 1990.

'The Lord is my shepherd; I shall not want. He maketh me to lie down in green pastures; He leadeth me beside the still waters.'

And I could almost hear the familiar names of the boys who were boys when I was a boy wafting over the lake in the evening breeze: Zamke, Shaike, Shmulik, Leipkaleh, Lazar, Welfke, *aheim der minute* ...

Notes

Some of the following information regarding survivors of Barovke was collected by Chaim on his visit to Israel shortly before his death.

Mendel Fleischman
(based on Chaim's notes, and interview with Elizabeth Olivestone)

Mendel was born in 1923. In 1934, he went to Yeshiva Ketana in Rezekne (near Barovke). In 1937, he went to Yeshiva Gedola in Dvinsk. He stayed there for four years, and was 18 when the Germans arrived. At the time, his father was hospitalized in Dvinsk but the hospital quickly emptied, due to the German invasion, and Mendel accompanied him back to Barovke.

He got a lift back to Dvinsk on a transporter lorry (which was used to transport children from the towns, to safety in the countryside). He stayed in Dvinsk for a few days, and then, together with a number of fellow students, fled by bicycle to the Russian border. The border was closed for a short while and when it re-opened on 3 July, they travelled to the nearest town with a railway station. From there, they took a train to Samarkand, on the other side of Russia. Mendel then travelled, via Siberia, to

Afghanistan, in the hope of eventually getting to Palestine. But he gave up after another group of travellers, also bound for Palestine, were given away by their guides, and never returned.

He moved to Riga in 1945, where he practised as a *felsher* (a paramedic) till 1979, when he emigrated to Israel. He now lives in Holon, and has three children, five grandchildren and a great-grandchild.

Fleischman remembers that Barovke burned down a few weeks before the German invasion – the fire started at the house of Bork Gandler, a butcher and cattle-dealer. The synagogue was miraculously saved. On 26 June 1941, the Jews were rounded up in the synagogue, and told they would be taken to the Breslev ghetto. Karl Zussman, a boy of 13 or 14, tried to escape and swam across the lake, only to be shot when he reached the other side.

According to Mendel Fleischman, there were 189 homes in Barovke:

80 consisted of one room.

45 consisted of two rooms.

38 of three rooms.

20 of four.

Six of five rooms.

There was also one house with over five rooms.

There was a shop in Barovke selling wine, beer and spirits – did extremely well, had a monopoly. Zamke Zmuskevitz, born in 1926, was the son of a tailor. Possibly the only son, he had five sisters, one of whom, Gittel Zmuskevitz, survived the war and is still living in Petach-Tikva, Israel.

Beirach Fleischman, Mendel's father, was also a tailor.

Abraham Pinkashovitz, the engineer, and his father, the wealthy owner of an oil refinery, died before the war.

Abrasha Zeitlin survived the war, but his two brothers and a sister were killed.

Dr Lapinski survived as he was away from Barovke when the Germans rounded up the Jews.

Moishe Yudeh's daughter, Feigele, was a *madricha* (youth leader) in Hashomer Hatzair, and married Beirach's son, Kalman.

Reuven Panz
(based on interview with Alisa Karban)

Reuven Panz, aged 76 (in 1998), was the son of Yaakov, a shoemaker. His grandfather, Aron, owned a hall which was used for all the weddings in the community. He had two brothers (one of whom had been a childhood friend of Chaim's) and three sisters.

He was born in Barovke, but in 1939, aged 18 years, he left to broaden his horizons in Riga, where he worked as an upholsterer.

In May 1941, Reuven was conscripted into the Red Army, and sent to Siberia. He ended up in Berlin, and at the end of the war in 1945, he returned to Barovke. There he discovered that all of his family had been killed. Only a cousin remained, who is still living in Riga today.

He went back to Riga, where he married, and in 1970, he emigrated to Israel. He settled in Kfar Ata, near the northern city of Haifa, where he still lives.

His first wife died in 1990, and a son, in December 1997. He has four grandchildren.

Reuven told Alisa that Chaim had seen a photograph showing youth from Hashomer Hatzair (the Labour Zionist youth movement) in Barovke, and was amazed that such a secular and political group existed in this tiny orthodox, provincial community. This seemed to conflict with his childhood memories.

Reuven explained that there had been little to do in Barovke, so that when Theodore Lynn, from Dvinsk, introduced the youth movement to the township, the youth welcomed it. They rented a house for their activities, and held bonfires on the festival of Lag B'omer. They supported the Zionist ideals of the movement, but were *not* irreligious – there were no secular Jews in Barovke.

He talked to Alisa about his fond memories of Chaim's father, Rabbi Azriel Bermant. He described him as very religious. A *talmid chacham* (a learned scholar), but very modest, and who disliked fanaticism.

He gave much respect to his students, and received great respect in return. He held an open house – anyone could come and go as they liked. He didn't place himself on a pedestal, but was a genuinely good man, with a warm heart. He never hit his students (which was a common practice, at that time, amongst teachers in the strictly orthodox community). He was a real *hassid* (righteous Jew), he was wise, quiet, humble and greatly loved.

This description tallies with Chaim's dedication to his father in his book *Coming Home*, where he describes him as, 'One of the world's 36 Just Men' – known as *lammed vovnicks*.

Of Chaim's mother, Feige Bermant, Reuven said, 'I didn't know her very well. She kept herself to herself, but she was well respected, and a good woman.'

He remembered that Feige's uncle in Glasgow, Louis Daets, had, for some time, been putting pressure on the family to leave Barovke. When they did leave, he recalled that they were given a huge and tearful send-off, as befitted a family so loved and esteemed by the community. [The memories of which were to sustain Chaim's parents during the bleaker moments of their 'exile' in Glasgow.]

Reuven recalls some 46 families from Barovke, and knows of about ten Jews from the community who survived the Holocaust.

When he returned to Barovke in 1945, he was told how the Jews were rounded up in the synagogue opposite the Fleischman house, and then taken to the forest outside town, where they were killed.

After the war, the survivors returned and erected a fence around the grave. They all contributed towards the cost of maintaining the grave and raising a monument to the memory of their loved ones. From then on, each year, on the first Sabbath after the fast of Tisha B'Av, they would hold a memorial service for the Jews of Barovke.

Reuven also gave Alisa the following information on the fate of the Barovke Jewish community, which he received from the Yad Vashem Holocaust Musem. They supplied information about the 115 people he could recall. The rest would have been young children whose names he could not remember.

1. Family Pinzov: four people killed.
2. Family Fleischman: parents and eight children killed. Two survived – Mendel, who lives in Israel, and Yitzhak, who lives in Gorky, Russia.
3. Family Trupin: family of six. Parents and four children killed, including Shaike, one of Chaim's childhood gang.
4. Family Panz: family of eight. Only Reuven survived. His brother, Leible, had been a childhood friend of Chaim's.
5. Birman – three families: fourteen killed. Three survived (Wolf, Shimon and Sima Birman).
6. Family Ellerin: eight members killed.
7. Family Zmuzkevitz: seven members of the family killed, including Chaim's childhood friend, Zamke (Zalman). Sheine Gittel still alive, in Petach-Tikva, Israel.
8. Family Gandler: four people killed.
9. Family Zubovitz: two people killed.
10. Family Leibowitz, including Boruch Sholem the 'Rothschild' of Barovke: three members killed.
11. Family Mendel: two members killed.
12. Family Pinkashovitz: (owned turpentine factory). Four members killed.
13. Family Yam: three members killed.
14. Family Shluper: three members killed.
15. Family Rosin: two members killed. One survivor, Sara Bluma Rosin.
16. Family Schlossberg: Mendel der schvartze – black-bearded Mendel. Six members killed.
17. Family Sandler: two members killed.
18. Family Zeitlin: seven members killed. One survivor, Abrasha Zeitlin.
19. Family Zilberman: four members killed.
20. Family Frost: four members killed. One survivor, Matis Frost.
21. Family Ritz: two members killed.
22. Family Goren: two members killed.
23. Family Ratz: (next-door neighbours of Chaim's family). Five members killed.

24. Family Munitz: two members killed.
25. Family Lynn: one member killed (probably Theodore, who introduced Hashomer Hatzair in Barovke). (Wife died earlier.)
26. Family Frankel: one member killed.
27. Family Segal: one member (Yitzke) killed.
28. Family Zack: three members killed.

List of survivors from Jewish Barovke
(those known to Reuven Panz)

1. Abrasha Zeitlin: lived in Riga (recently deceased).
2. Mendel Fleischman: living in Holon, Israel.
3. Yitzhak Fleischman (brother of Mendel): living in Gorky, Russia.
4. Sheine Gittel Zmuskevitz (or Shmushkevitz): Petach-Tikva, Israel.
5. Wolf Birman: living in Hod Hasharon, Israel.
6. Shimon Birman (brother of Wolf): lived in Riga (deceased).
7. Sima Birman (cousin of Shimon and Wolf): still alive, probably in Riga.
8. Matis Frost: living in Rishon Lezion, Israel.
9. Sara Bluma Rosin: lived in Riga (deceased).
10. Reuven Panz: living in Kiriat Ata, near Haifa, Israel.
11. Rosa Kastrel: living in Haifa, Israel.
12. Gela Kastrel: lived in Germany (deceased).
13. Boruch Steiman: living in Riga.
14. Motke Kit: living in Riga.
15. Gershon Zubovitch (deceased).
16. Moshe Zubovitch (deceased).

Memories

By Danny Bermant

Last month, I found myself fulfilling a responsibility that, previously, I had never even tried to imagine – making the preparations for my father's funeral. It was only a few hours after his passing, and the enormity of what had just happened hadn't yet sunk in. I was dreading the following day. I had attended funerals before, and found them quite upsetting. How could I face laying to rest someone who only the previous day had been part of my everyday life? As the funeral drew closer, I grew more and more nervous. Azi and Alisa, my brother and sister who flew in from Israel, arrived only an hour beforehand. We all rushed to get ready. The *Chevra Kedisha* finally arrived, the Psalms were recited. It was time for my father to depart for the last time.

But as the funeral procession began, my feelings changed. As we walked down Hill Rise, I remembered my father's daily morning walk down to the market place for his cigarettes and newspapers. And during the drive to Bushey Cemetery, north of London, although we felt terribly sad, we were also laughing and joking about many of the funny things that my father had said and done. When Rabbi Jackson gave his eulogy, it included some humorous references and that's about the only time I've heard laughter at a funeral. As we left Bushey, I felt a little more positive about the afternoon's events. It had not been the scene of despair that I had anticipated, but a celebration of my father's life.

During the *Shiva*, we were visited by literally hundreds of people. I have felt slightly guilty about the fact that whilst many of those visiting us were tearful and speechless, we often found ourselves laughing and joking. I like to think that we have inherited my father's sense of humour, and find it a consolation that aspects of his personality live on in us. He made me realize how important it is to have a sense of humour, even at times of sorrow. It enables you to see everything in proportion. And my father had the ability to see the lighter side of almost any situation.

I also began to feel positive for other reasons. Although dad was sometimes criticized for causing communal divisions through his outspoken views, his funeral was attended by representatives from right across the community. It was surely a testament to him that rabbis from every denomination (Reform, Conservative, United Synagogue, and the Ultra Orthodox) were present. And on the political spectrum, there were those from the left to the right. My father could connect to a diverse range of people, because he had a remarkable ability to separate individuals from their opinions. And they in turn admired him for the courage of his convictions.

My father stood up for his beliefs, even if it meant alienating those who considered themselves to be his supporters. At the 1996 Limmud Conference, my father gave a session entitled 'At Large in the Media'. He felt he was misunderstood. Whilst the press were often guilty of printing what they thought you wanted to read, readers were often guilty of demanding opinions that they agreed with. He said that it was the job of the columnist to be a maverick, and question the dominant view of the newspaper. My father said that when he read a columnist, he wanted to have his prejudices challenged, rather than confirmed. Clearly, he possessed a level of intellectual maturity that many in the community lacked.

About 18 months ago, my father criticized gay commitment ceremonies that were being carried out by a progressive rabbi. Following the publication of this article, many liberal-minded readers, who previously considered him to be 'one of them' wrote in to complain that he had betrayed them. It was so typical of my father, that whilst many in the Jewish community regarded him as being too liberal in his religious and Zionist views, in the wider community he was often considered too right wing to be given a platform. When asked if he had any reservations about the Jewish press in this country, he said he regretted that there was no decent right-wing commentator to oppose him. He was unchallenged, and that bothered him.

I often found it difficult to understand those who regarded him as anti-religious. When it comes to judging how religious a person is, the ones who have the most right to speak are those closest to that person. Dad believed in the concept of 'serving God with Joy' – that observing Judaism with your heart, rather than being obsessed with halachic detail, was what really mattered. He loved Jewish rituals and customs, and encouraged us to enjoy them. I'll never forget how my father treated *bedikat chametz* (the search for leaven before Passover) as though we were searching some haunted house. While Azi and I were meticulously searching through the cupboards of one room, my father had already completed searching the whole house. He liked to do things quickly. When it came to *gemilut chasadim*, acts of loving kindness, my father always put himself out for others. And when it came to speaking out on social issues, he was often a lone voice.

As I walked to *shul* with Azi on the Shabbat following the funeral, we both felt so vulnerable. I thought about a talk the Chief Rabbi once gave. He was visiting a kindergarten and asking the children what they liked the most about Shabbat. When he asked one small child what it meant to her, she said: 'It's the only time I get to see daddy.'

Dad loved Shabbat – its relaxed atmosphere, the break from his weekly routine – and it was also my favourite day of the week, partly because it meant spending time with him. I always enjoyed walking to *shul*, drinking, eating, and chatting with him, as well as accompanying him to *shiurim*. He wasn't always such a great talker or listener, but I always felt he was there. We got on extremely well.

While many people my age left home years ago, I was quite proud of the fact that I was still living with my parents. I loved inviting friends to lunch on Shabbat. I thought that my father was a great entertainer and my mother a superb cook. Between them, they made a great team. In fact, one of my friends felt embarrassed about the affectionate way in which my parents would often look at each other at the table. My mother was always so devoted to dad. With both of them working from home, she would often proof-read his articles and manuscripts before publication. And she often checked on his progress when he was working under the pressure of tight deadlines.

I'll miss the little things about my father. He always washed up during the week, and you could tell, because half the dinner was left on the plates. I'll miss being his driver (whenever he went to a social function, he wanted to have a few drinks). And I'll miss his humorous comments, such as the one he made about a certain synagogue in north-west London, many of whose congregants had been found guilty of tax evasion: 'Half of them have done time, the other half should have done time.' It was the kind of comment that only he could get away with. My father was larger than life. He was a constant presence at home, and was the centre of attention. Now he's gone, the house suddenly feels very large and unprotected.

Still, he has left so much behind. I'm glad that I've inherited his beliefs, his values, his love of life, and something of his sense of fun. I have many fond memories that no one can take away from me, and most of all, I have my mother, Alisa, Evie and Azi. I think we all of us have a bit of dad in us. Above all, I feel immense pride of the fact that Chaim Bermant was my father.

By Evie Bermant

The last time I spoke to my father was on the phone to Israel, where he had gone to do research for the final chapter of this book. My sister, Alisa, had phoned up for a chat, and, since dad was staying with her at the time, she called him over to have a quick word. I can remember thinking that it wasn't necessary, since he'd be home in a few days, and we could 'catch up' then.

Perhaps I found phone calls with my father a little unsatisfactory, for I tended to defer proper conversation till we ·could speak in person. A typical exchange on the phone might go as follows:

> Dad: Evie! (incomprehensible exclamation of surprise) How are things?
> Evie: Okay, I suppose.
> Dad: Any news? How's school?
> Evie: Dad, I've given up teaching, remember.
> Dad: Oh, so you have. Keeping yourself out of mischief then?
> Evie: I s'pose so.
> Dad: Want to speak to your muvver?

Looking back, it was immensely touching how, no matter how regularly I saw or spoke to him, daddy always sounded so surprised and delighted to hear from me. It was as if he couldn't quite believe in the powers of that technological miracle, the telephone. But we rarely spoke on the phone for long, and, after initial greetings had been exchanged, he would generally pass me over to my mother, or 'the guv'nor', as he invariably called her. I must admit that I often wasn't very forthcoming myself, assuming that dad was too preoccupied by his writing to want to listen to my bits of news. Now, I can see that I was unfair, because, while he might not always have shown it overtly, he cared enormously about all of us and took an avid interest in whatever was happening in our lives. The fact is, although a man of words, daddy was never a great conversationalist, and this became most apparent to me when talking to him on the phone.

In retrospect, I feel so grateful to Alisa for insisting that I speak to dad there and then, rather than waiting till he was home, for now I treasure that phone call and keep replaying it in my mind. Little did I know, then, that it was the last time I would speak to him.

And because I was unaware, at the time, of the huge significance of that conversation, I did not 'hang on' to dad's every word, or make any attempt to prolong the call. Of course, I knew that this particular visit to Israel was deeply important to him, as he was there in order to meet a handful of survivors from Barovke, whom he hadn't seen for sixty years. I vaguely remember asking about them, and that dad didn't reveal much, apart from, 'Poor chap – wasn't much use, because he wasn't all there', about the man he had met that day, and criticizing the food he was served (food was a constant theme). But, again, I wasn't too disappointed because I knew he would have plenty to tell us when he got back, and so didn't persist in questioning him. He then told me all about my sister's new house, praised its view and location, and described the antics of his beloved grandchildren. I also seem to recall him mentioning that he had a stomach upset, but I wasn't too worried, because he sounded fine, and who on earth would worry about a mere stomach ache?

Of course, now I am kicking myself for not being more concerned about his state of health and begging him to look after himself, for not pressing him with searching questions and insisting on detailed answers, for not prolonging the conversation, for not remembering every word he said, for not taping the call ... But then, how was I, or anyone, to know what would happen less than a week later?

I can recall feeling a little uneasy about dad's impulsive decision to go to Israel, as soon as he heard about the Barovke survivors, and can only imagine that that was because he had never been much good at taking care of himself. Since we were very young, Alisa and I, in particular, worried about dad's health and feared that something might happen to him, especially if mum wasn't there to watch over him. From time to time, dad did go away on his own, but, for some reason, none of us was ever very happy at the idea and we were always so relieved when he came back 'in one piece'.

Thinking back, it is interesting how, in our case, the traditional Jewish parent/child roles were sometimes reversed. I remember, some years ago, waiting up late for my father to get home from a party – my mother was away at the time – and wondering if I should call the police. (It turned out that he had had rather a lot to drink, and had to wait for a lift home, a not untypical scenario.) I felt a bit like 'James James Morrison Morrison Weatherby George Dupree/(who) took great care of his mother although he was only three' from the A. A. Milne poem.

There must have been something rather vulnerable about him – no doubt, connected with his smoking and drinking habits, and generally excessive lifestyle – which was why we were often so fearful and protective over him. Perhaps I was particularly uneasy in this case, because he was in the middle of writing his autobiography – possibly his masterpiece – and there was the tiny, but nagging fear that he mightn't get to finish it. I remember telling a friend that his book was due to come out in the spring, and how excited I was about it, and then feeling that I shouldn't be counting my (or, rather, dad's) chickens, before they had hatched. At the time, I knew that the book was almost at the 'hatching' stage, but still felt that I couldn't make any assumptions about its completion, and that to do so, was tempting fate.

I realize that this way of thinking is rather superstitious, even primitive, yet it is oddly apt, for somehow it suggests the legacy of my father's old-world *shtetl* upbringing, so beautifully evoked in these pages.

By Alisa Karban

It was Malka (one of my father's few remaining cousins) who called with the news. 'There are survivors: Mendel Fleischman, formerly of Barovke, is living here in Israel. He remembers Chaim's family very well.'

My mother (there at the time on a visit) and I jumped for joy. Unbelievable. From what my father understood, all the Jews had been killed. My mother's eyes welled up with tears as she listened enraptured to Mendel Fleischman's description of my *zeider* (grandfather). 'He was my rebbe, the first to teach me Torah. What a wonderful kind warm man!' My *zeider* (my father's father, Reb Azriel Baruch Bermant) had died at my parents' engagement. They were always saying how sad they were that he never lived to see us. Even though I never knew him, his presence was felt very much. My father, I believe, inherited many of his characteristics.

On hearing that there were survivors now living in Israel, my father made plans on the spot to come out the very next week. My mother had her reservations about his going. She had visions of him getting on and off stuffy Egged Buses, travelling from one end of Israel to the other, not leaving time to rest, not looking after himself (which he never did anyway). She was worried about him becoming over-excited and over-emotional (which of course he was), and she tried to get him to put it off till later on when she could accompany him. But my father was adamant. Through Mendel Fleischman, other survivors had been discovered, including an old lady of 90 and who knows how long she'd last out. He had to go now, there was no turning back.

My father's stay in Israel was a very emotional one for him. He was greeted with open arms, tears and with many long lost memories. The last time he saw these people was when he was nine years old and here they were together again 60 years on. Most thought he was the image of his late father. They in fact saw 'their rebbe' in him. Most of them were not observant Jews – many had fled to different cities during the war, keeping their Judaism a closely guarded secret. A few had married outside the religion, and their children had very little knowledge of their Jewish heritage. When they learned of my father's visit, they went out of their way to ensure that all the food was kosher, and prepared a huge feast. He felt that he had no choice but to partake.

As my father moved from person to person, he discovered at each point another Barovke survivor (a total of six). He met up with four of them, but kept returning to get more information. Each person had a different story, and a different viewpoint. He toyed with the idea of staying an extra week, but was anxious to get back to his study and get it down in writing, in the comfortable familiar surroundings that he loved so much.

My father was terribly excited and gave me vivid descriptions and stories of the people he had met. We had already said goodbye on Thursday evening, but then he discovered a certain Reuven Gershon Panz living in Kfar Ata in Haifa, who, he was told, could explain what happened to most of the people who lived in Barovke. On Saturday evening, my father returned to our house in Haifa. As soon as he walked through the door, he complained that he was feeling poorly, and by next morning, his condition had worsened. But only after much persuasion did he agree to go for a check-up at the city's main hospital.

'I passed the test,' he later told me when he called to say goodbye from Ben Gurion Airport. 'And how was your visit to Reuven Panz?' I asked. 'Difficult,' he answered. 'I wasn't feeling well but it was worth it. We had a lot of catching up to do.' That was the last time I spoke to him. Little did I know that three days later, I would be saying my final farewell at his funeral.

After the Shivah, we went through his diary, books and travel bag, but we could find little relating to his visit. We found a few old photographs and some notes, but there was a lot of missing information. Maybe he had it all in his head and intended to put it down on paper when he returned.

When I returned to Israel, the first thing I did was to retrace my father's footsteps. He had spoken about most of the people that he had met up with, but he never got a chance to write of his encounter with Reuven Panz. He must have been important, because of the 'heroic' effort (his exact words) that my father made to see him.

Despite my terrible sense of direction, I made my way to Reuven Panz's house without once stopping to ask the way. I really felt as though my father was guiding me there. There was a sweet little cat waiting for me outside the house who then followed me inside (a sure sign that it was the right house. My father loved cats.) A small bespectacled man in his mid-seventies, wearing a black beret, opened the door. He nodded without saying a word and let me into a very modest and bare sitting room. He sat across to me in silence and waited for me to speak. I couldn't get the words out and started to cry, at which point so did he. (He had been told of my father's death only the previous week.) His wife, a large motherly Russian woman, gave me a big hug and wiped my tears, comforting me in Russian or maybe Yiddish.

After a bit, we both calmed down and I asked him to tell me about my father's visit. He told me of how my father had called him up, saying that he was Chaim Bermant, originally from Barovke, and he had answered, 'What my rebbe's son?' When my father entered the house, his initial reaction was to say, 'Rebbe, your beard has turned grey!' though, of course, he knew that my zeder was dead and this was in fact my father. He told me that my father wanted to know what had happened to the people he had grown up with. Most of them, tragically, had died in the Holocaust. He gave me all the information he had given my father and I, in turn, read him the account that he wrote in the *Jewish Chronicle* ('Return to Barovke'). He couldn't believe how much my father remembered, and with such detail and clarity.

'But how can a nine-year-old child remember so much? After all I was 18 at the time.' As I continued the account, tears rolled down his cheeks. He kept shaking his head in disbelief.

I know how dearly my father treasured the memories of Barovke, and how much it meant to him to be able to meet its few survivors – particularly as, till so recently, he hadn't even known of any. It gives us some comfort that he had the opportunity to see them again, and to share their recollections of life in *der heim*. And for me, it meant a great deal that, during dad's recent visit to Israel, I had the chance to see him – and my children to see their grandfather – before he died.

By Azriel Bermant

It is hard to believe that a month has passed since dad came to see me in Jerusalem. I remember that I had arranged for him to come over at 2.30 pm and felt a little nervous before he turned up – possibly because I hadn't seen him for some time.

When dad turned up, he seemed in reasonable health, although he complained of feeling a little sick from the bus journey. We walked down to San Simon to go apartment hunting. Our agent took us to see four apartments, only one of which we really liked.

We then went out for a coffee at the patisserie across the road from me. Sadly, this was the last time he would take me out. Now, every time I go past it, I look at the table where we sat, and am reminded of him.

When we returned home, dad made a number of phone calls to various Barovke survivors whom he had only recently found out about. (He had previously assumed that all of the town's Jewish inhabitants had perished in the Holocaust.) There was one man, in particular, whom he was eager to meet – Reuven Panz, who had clear recollections of my paternal grandfather (my *zeidah*), his rabbi and teacher in Barovke.

Dad and I spent that Shabbat at my aunt and uncle's in Rehovot. On the Friday evening we went to *shul* together and I can recall dad perusing a sheet on the Sedrah (weekly Torah portion) distributed by the Lubavitch movement, and, characteristically, dismissing it as 'a load of drivel'!

That night, there was a party going on a couple of streets away, and the noise was appalling. All you could hear was a pneumatic thump, thump, and loads of screaming – no doubt bearing out all of dad's prejudices about rowdy Israeli teenagers and popular music – and we hardly slept a wink.

Dad obviously wasn't himself on the Shabbat. His eyes looked very red and, more to the point, he turned down the offer of whisky, saying, 'The very sight of it makes me feel sick.' To which my uncle responded, 'In that case you really must be ill!' But if dad was very sick, he was hiding it from us.

He ate very little during lunch, even refusing the *cholent*, which was normally one of his favourite dishes. During the meal I can clearly remember him joking about his 'snuffing it' before he could repay the money he owed my uncle! (Typical of dad's sense of humour.) Maybe he knew something we didn't?'

Despite feeling unwell on the Saturday night, dad decided to go up to Haifa in order to meet Reuven Panz.

My uncle gave us both a lift, but he dropped me off first, and I will never forget saying goodbye to dad. As I left the car, he hurriedly lowered the window and held out his hand for me to shake. In retrospect, it was almost as though he knew we were seeing each other for the last time.

My father would be returning to England on the Sunday evening. My sister, Alisa, phoned to find out if he had called, but he hadn't, and I started to feel a little anxious that maybe something had happened. To my relief he called me later that afternoon to say goodbye. This was the last time I would ever speak to him.

I settled back into my busy routine, and, as far as I knew, I had no reason to worry about dad. I was glad that he was going back to England, as he hadn't been feeling well, and that he could get down to finishing off his book.

On the Tuesday morning, I heard on the news that Zevulun Hammer, the education minister, had passed away, and remember telling my flatmate, Jonathan, about it. Little was I to know that, only a few hours later, I would be hearing the same news about my father.

Later that morning, I got a message that Alisa had called. I then got a second message in the afternoon that I should call her urgently. I was shaken. I feared the worst and called my sister, but the line was busy. Eventually I got through, and I will never forget her words: 'Azi ... are you sitting down? I have some very bad news ... Daddy has died.'

Alisa's voice was soft, as though to lessen the impact of the blow. I remember closing my eyes and trying to pretend I had imagined the whole thing, that it was some kind of nightmare. But no, it was real, and somehow I had to face it.

It was little consolation, but I was so glad that at least I had seen daddy a few days previously. I have fresh memories of going to look at apartments with him, and going out for a *cappuccino*. I also felt it was appropriate that dad should have spent his last days with the survivors of Barovke, the place where he had been brought up. In this way, his life had come full circle.